Donna's Day

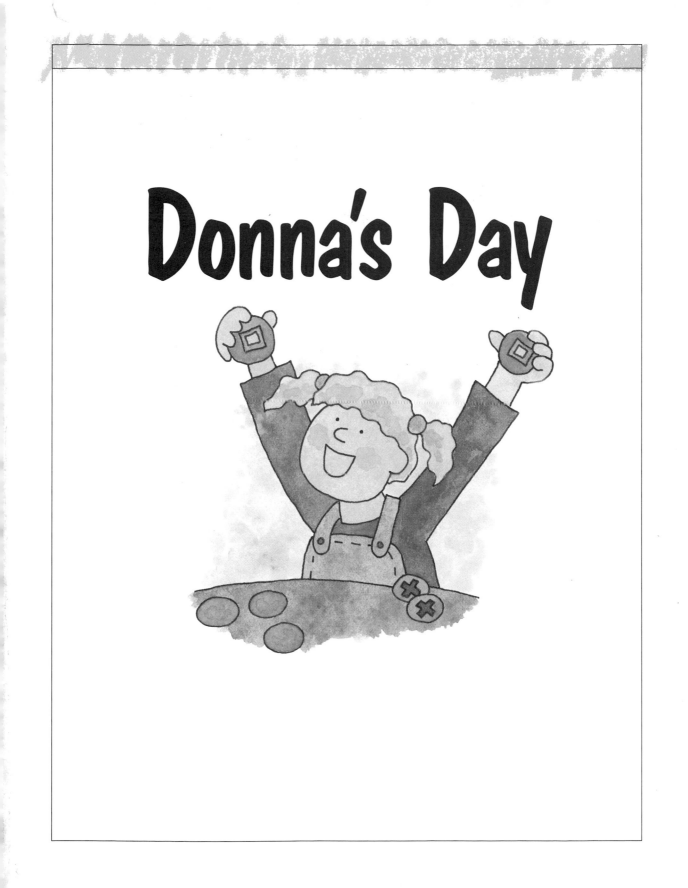

Donna's Day

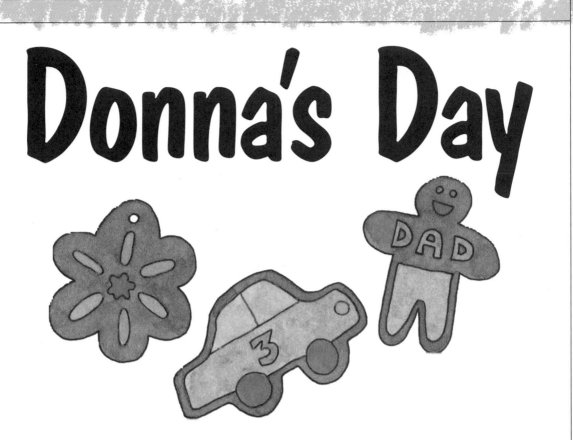

FUN ACTIVITIES THAT BRING THE FAMILY TOGETHER

Donna Erickson
ILLUSTRATIONS BY DAVID LAROCHELLE

HarperCollins*Publishers*

DONNA'S DAY. Copyright © 1998 by Prime Time with Kids, Inc. All rights reserved. Printed in the United States of America. No part of this book may be used or reproduced in any manner whatsoever without written permission except in the case of brief quotations embodied in critical articles and reviews. For information address HarperCollins Publishers, Inc., 10 East 53rd Street, New York, NY 10022.

HarperCollins books may be purchased for educational, business, or sales promotional use. For information please write: Special Markets Department, HarperCollins Publishers, Inc., 10 East 53rd Street, New York, NY 10022.

FIRST EDITION

Designed by Charles Kreloff

ISBN 0–06–019111–2

98 99 00 ❖ RRD 10 9 8 7 6 5 4 3 2 1

To the person who has taught me the importance of tradition
and togetherness, and who continues to make the idea
of family real . . . my mom, Dolly Anduri.

Contents

Atlas in the Kitchen 65

Hikes and Bikes (and Car Trips Too) 89

Rollicking Rituals to Run the House 105

Family Connections 127

A Mess a Minute 147

Acknowledgments

My thanks to my editor Mauro DiPreta and his staff at HarperCollins for their enthusiasm and skill in bringing the philosophy and activities of Donna's Day from television to book form. Special thanks to Meg Schneider who helped write the activities, making them as fun to read as they are to do. To illustrator David LaRochelle whose wit and sensitivity invite adults and children to the activities, and to designer Charles Kreloff.

Thanks to the *Donna's Day* television production team. In particular, Hugh Martin, director of *Donna's Day*, whose vision, creativity, and tireless effort have provided tremendous support for me. Also, Lonnie Porro, Gerry Richman, Colleen Miner for her culinary ideas, Rick Hauser, Lisa Burkhart, Mike Phillips, Anna Gingerich, Sheryl Shade, Arthur Novell, Maggie Begly and Melissa Cohen. And special thanks to Ken Powell at General Mills and Bridget Boel and Madeline Boyer at Time-Life Kids.

Thanks to friends, relatives and coworkers for their creativity and generosity: Maria Carmicino at King Features Syndicate, Ann Pleshette Murphy and Wendy Smolen at *Parents* Magazine, Rod Eaton and Debbie Estes at Target, Jill Johnson at Tunheim Santrizos, Cynthia McGovern and her students at Minnehaha Academy, Suzanne Phillips, Deborah Orenstein, Frank Weimann, Mark Lambeck, Phyllis Erickson, Rev. Don Johnson, Jeannie Klint, Lorna McLearie, Rebecca Anderson, Anne Ahlem, and Terri Swanson.

Finally, thanks to my husband, Dean Erickson, and our children, Bjorn, Britt, and Anders who through play, encouragement, and bright ideas have supported this project from its beginning.

A Note on Creativity and Safety

All the activities in this book are designed so that kids and adults can work together every step of the way. Younger children will need a bit more supervision, of course, accompanied by lots of enthusiastic encouragement. They may need extra help as they try to manipulate scissors, string beads, or create templates.

However, there are moments when an adult should take over. This is particularly so in the kitchen, where hot pans, pots, and oil could easily burn eager fingers. Sharp scissors and knives are also potentially dangerous, and depending on the age of your child might, require your hands alone. Keep an eye out for those moments when an adult's help might ease the way or avert an accident.

So, be cautious but supportive. Let your kids expand their skills as much as possible by assisting you. Eventually they will be ready to stand safely over a frying pan and will best learn how to do so in your company.

You've Got What It Takes!

Let's face it. Family life is about 90 percent chaos. But amid all the busyness and confusion remains one unshakable truth. Kids are our priority, our most important responsibility, and our greatest joy. They are what we care about most. And it's the little things we do that really count: a hug on the way to school, a vote of confidence before a big test, an "I'm so happy to see you" when they walk in the door. These gestures help build a home on rock-solid ground.

No matter what the day is like, you and your child can find time to enjoy yourselves while building a wonderful and trusting relationship. Look for opportunities to connect with your kids. I sometimes have those moments with my kids in the car while we're driving to basketball games, or when we're simply tossing the salad for dinner, or when we're scurrying around in the morning and I say, "Honey, let's make breakfast," while extending the marmalade jar, a little spoon, and a piece of toast.

So move through your day with an eye toward sharing the everyday moments. I mean, do you have to press the button on the coffee grinder yourself? No. Imagine what pleasure your child might have doing it with you. As it spins, you can say, "Goodness, what else sounds like that?" And she might answer, as you begin eating breakfast, "It's a little like the drill they were using on the street corner!" And you might add, "Also when something big gets all ground up in the garbage disposal."

And before you know it, you've connected, got each other thinking, smiled a lot, and, well, *that's what counts!*

Here are some other moments in everyday routines you might want to try taking advantage of, and a few little hints for conversation starters:

👋 *Matching socks from the laundry basket:* "Which socks are the same color?" "This texture feels different from that, doesn't it?" "Where do you imagine the missing socks go?"

👋 *Helping your child shampoo:* "How many different hairdos can we make?" you might say as you fashion her locks.

👋 *Sewing on buttons:* Have your child choose the color thread: "That would look nice. Which color do you think would be the weirdest combination?"

👋 *Clipping coupons together:* "What do you think we could do with the money we save?"

👋 *Putting away the silverware:* "Do you know there are lots of countries where people don't eat with these? Here's what they do. . . . "

So whether you are putting away those mementos from the summer in a fun way with a MEMORY LAUNDRY LINE, splashing around in a FAMILY BIKE WASH, or giving vent to a creative spurt on POTATO GEM JEWELRY, this book shows you how to make these more than just, well, activities. They can set the stage for building communication opportunities between adults and children and provide a great arena for your child to experience success, feel his own strengths, and sharpen all kinds of skills. This important time shared builds a lifetime of supply of family "glue."

Beyond doing the activities is the satisfaction of enjoying what you have created. In our home, hatboxes we decorated hold the children's toys. Our houseplants grow in terracotta planters they painted, and in the kitchen our placemats are laminated color photocopies of their designs. The kids feel the space is really a reflection of who they are.

The added bonus, of course, is that we've done these things together. And that's what it's all about. It's the little things we do that yield big results.

Yes, your children will remember the big trips to an amusement park, but it's the small day-to-day moments of family life that create the real sense of being loved and belonging.

Being the Resident Artist Is the Least of It

If you are trying to say, "Honey, I love being with you," to your child in new and different ways, these activities are for you. If you want to put a little time aside to just do something pleasurable with your children, these activities are for you. And if you genuinely want to keep in touch with what's on their minds and in their hearts, then these activities are perfect for you.

Other than the above skills, you need to be able to handle the following sorts of jobs:

❦ Cut vegetables and dunk them in paint.

❦ Cut paper into weird shapes and wield a glue brush.

❦ Pick up leaves and twigs on the ground.

❦ Stick almond slivers into already prepared marzipan.

❦ Photocopy old photographs (press buttons).

❦ Stick your hands in goopy stuff.

Do you see my point? You are a parent who wants to have fun with your children. That's all it takes.

As for the activities themselves and the specific creative details, that's why you have this book. I'll offer ideas to get you started. The basics. And a few alternatives.

But trust yourself. You'll want to give things your own spin too.

For instance, I suggest cutting up vegetables and dipping them in paint and then stamping them on cut-up paper bags to make wrapping paper. As an alternative, I also mention dunking the wheels of your kids' old little cars into the paint, and rolling those over the paper.

But maybe you can think of something else. The bottoms of baby shoes? Sure. Maybe thumbprints? Why not. Especially if your kids are in a messy mood. Maybe they would like walking across the paper in bare painted feet?

And then there're always fall leaves, homemade paw prints. . . .

See Your Home Through Different Glasses

Okay, let's get a little more specific. You'll see in a moment that your home is really no different from mine. You simply have to look at things through another filter. "Different glasses." Think of how you can use an ordinary thing for something other than its intended use. Suddenly the most mundane, disposable objects take on such amazing possibilities:

Brown paper bags for garlands or wrapping paper

Milk cartons for candles or bird feeders

Buttons and lace off old clothes for decorating anything

Old garden gloves for a glamorous new look

Old jeans pockets as a catchall glued anywhere

Blooper or unused family photos for posters and wrapping paper

Crayon stubs for making crazy crayon shapes

Plastic lids from margarine tubs for stencils

Empty food jars for snow globes or butter making

Plain paper plates for spin art

Clear adhesive paper for nature bracelets

Yarn for stringing, trimming, tying anything!

Plastic bottles for scoop toys

Old shoe bags for over-the-car-seat toy holders

Cereal boxes for making a puzzle

Faded old curtains for costumes

Plastic six-pack collars for a super bubbler

Pinecones outside your door for firestarters

Ribbons off opened gifts for trim

Tissue paper (all colors) for votive candles

Tin coffee cans for candle making

Hangers for paper plate mobiles

It's not that I don't like cleaning up and throwing things out. I do. Every fall, right after camp and before school begins, I like to go through my kids' rooms and start tossing out all the stuff they never touch but that keeps piling up.

It's just that usually somewhere buried under the empty toy space ship box, or a small pile of crumpled line paper, is a potential treasure.

This might be a good time to stop and show you my tried-and-true guidelines for things that look ready for the trash. Before you throw anything out, think . . .

❦ If it gets wet, will it fall apart? If not, save it.

❦ Is it colorful, and can it be cut up? If yes, save it.

❦ Does it hold special memories? If so, save it.

❦ Is the shape unusual, or does it have an interesting texture or pattern? Well, definitely save that!

Then place the big stuff in a giant box (I call it my recycling bin) and the smaller doo-dah stuff sorted out into a junk drawer and smaller boxes in one designated place. Maybe you can select a cupboard that the kids will know as Project Parts.

JUST GLU IT WHITE GLUE

That way, when you're ready to go, you'll just open the junk drawer for the little things, pull out the recycling bin for the big things, and then get to having fun.

The Supply Side: A Minimum of Fuss and Bother

You might be thinking, "Well, Donna has all her supplies ready, and she gets going, and it's done. But I have to look everywhere, get something down from this closet, another from that closet, and then I have to go shopping, and before I know it I'll have no time left!"

Well, that's just not so. Yes, you might want to spend a little time organizing things ahead of time. But you really only need to do that once.

Keep an Eye out While Shopping for . . .

Many of the activities in this book can be done with stuff you've either got around the house or were about to throw out. But, of course, lots of activities require an item or two you may not have on your shelves.

These things aren't hard to find. Most are basic standbys. You just need to tuck a few items in the back of your mind so that when you're in or near the appropriate place (hardware, grocery, crafts, discount clothing stores, tag or garage sale), you can pick up a few things without adding a trip to your already busy day:

Discount lamp shades

Waterproof glue

Acrylic paints in little jars

Squeeze bottles of fabric paint

Poster paints

Poster boards

Craft wire

Yards of ribbon

Old record player (garage sales are great for this item!)

Bricks of paraffin

Sandpaper

Glitter, feathers, sequins

Borax powder

Plain white T-shirts (discount stores)

. . . and anything else that strikes your fancy. Let your imagination run wild!

Take a look at the activities that intrigue you the most, make a mental note (or an actual note) of what you might need, and then just see where you find yourself on any given day.

Pretty soon you'll be ready for any of these activities.

Of course, the same may not be true for your kids!

There's No Right Way

Kids being the way they are, and life being the way it is, not everything goes "according to plan" every time you sit down to enjoy an activity together.

But then, I never liked that approach anyway.

It's one thing to watch me on television; gathering all the materials, going through the steps, flashing finished products here and there.

But when you get started, things are bound to be a little different. You'll be sitting around the room with your own kids and maybe some of their friends. You could find yourself listening to, "Wait! Not so fast!" or, "I'm thirsty! Let's stop. I need a drink!" or, "Hey! Mine's not turning out the way I want it to!" or, "I'm not gonna do this if you keep hogging all the glue!"

Be prepared for a few twists in the creative road. Anything from kids who don't like to get themselves too messy to older kids who say, "Nah, too babyish."

Maybe your child is in a good mood. Maybe he's not. Maybe he's feeling ready for anything, maybe he needs things "just so" in order to feel good. Or maybe he's one of those kids whose attention wanders. He starts decorating his picture frame and then says, "I don't know. I'm tired. I'll do the rest later."

So what do you do?

You remember that things don't have to be just so!

Maybe these suggestions will help:

If your child seems a little reluctant at first: Sometimes kids need to see what they're getting into before they commit! They may be hesitant about trying something new. Just sit down, lay out the "workplace," and start doing SALAD SPIN ART. Talk a little to yourself out loud as you do. "This is fun. I love how surprising it is." Affix the paper plate inside the spinner, drop a few dots of paint on the surface of the plate, cover up, and crank away. When it's done, take it out with a "Wow! How neat!" Hold it up for your child to see.

Seconds later she's sure to be spinning right next to you.

And if for some reason your child just doesn't seem interested after your most enthusiastic attempts? Well, maybe you caught her at the wrong time. Put it away and try again later.

If your child peers down at his T-shirt in mid–paint job, frowns, and says, "Ugh, I don't like it!": If you think it's beautiful, say so. If you too think it has problems, think of a way to fix it together. Sometimes a quick line here or a few dots there can turn a blob that was supposed to be a car into a magnificent-looking ladybug!

If your child stops in the middle of decorating a bead lamp and announces, "I've had enough": See if she's gotten stuck on some project step. Perhaps the wires aren't bending the way she'd like and she's a bit frustrated. But if it does seem as if she's simply run out of energy, then you may want to let her be. Which doesn't mean you have to grind to a halt. In fact, if she hangs around and watches you, it could help when she goes back to finishing her own lamp. Going from "A" to "Z" but ending with a frown is not nearly as important as getting from "A" to "G" with smiles all the way.

If your 12-year-old takes a look at the sponge-print wrapping paper and proclaims, "Sorry. Too babyish": Adolescence. Reminds me of a story about my preteen with whom I was walking one day. I innocently broke into a soft song. "Mom," he said, annoyed. "Please stop singing! It's embarrassing!" I was amazed. I looked at him, "But, honey," I said. "I feel so good. It's a beautiful day, and it's so nice to be with you!" He shrugged. "Okay," he whispered. "Fine. Just don't sing!"

So, okay, I say to you. But just don't stop the fun. Do things a little differently is all. Has he been wanting to redo his room? Make it for an "older" boy?

Why not cut sponges into shapes that mean something to him? Not stars. Maybe guitars. Not circles. Maybe hockey sticks. Give him a blank white lamp shade and let him create. In fact, attach a blank border to a wall in his room and encourage him to have a good time. And, of course, don't forget to offer to help.

If your child isn't interested in helping to plan for a trip: "Boring," she says. But what if she could choose the family's itinerary for that day? Or if she had a choice of two stopovers on the way to the destination, what would they be and what could the family do there? If she enjoys horseback riding or miniature golf, she could research the stables or courses in the area.

What am I saying? Be flexible. It's the kind of understanding that will keep you communicating about the big stuff . . . and the small.

Little Moments: A Lifetime of Memories

Some of you might be thinking to yourselves, "I don't know of a single day that's coming up in which I'd have time to do *any* of these activities!"

Life always has a way of changing. Hopefully, a little time will open up here and there. But if it doesn't, the most important thing to keep in mind is what I said at the very beginning.

The *Very* Little Moments Count Too

The unplanned, spontaneous times when you can share a hug or a laugh or . . . thaaaaaaaat's right! . . . an activity that is already built into your busy day.

I remember when my kids were really young and we would be so exhausted at the end of the day. My daughter would say, "Mom, can I paint your face? You look so tired!" So I'd put my head back, and she'd say, "Pretend my finger is a paintbrush." Then she'd gently paint one eyebrow and then the other. She'd paint my cheeks and ears and . . .

There were no words, but I felt a wonderful closeness that's hard to describe. It's important to recognize and enjoy a loving moment, even when it's brief and oh so silent.

Remember, your children want to be with you. They bask in your attention. It's certainly obvious with the little ones. But even older kids, who may sometimes appear uninterested as they reach for more and more independence, feel a sense of security knowing you love them and want to be a strong presence in their lives.

Every parent has something to share, and it's the memories of these shared gifts that will last a lifetime in your children's minds. Not only do you have your own life stories, but there are all the little and big pieces of knowledge unique to you that only you can teach. From explaining the different grades of sandpaper in a toolbox to preparing and creating favorite recipes in the kitchen, they all become insights and traditions that are passed on to children and help a family grow. Yes! Your life, loves, skills, experiences, and enthusiasms make you a dynamite parent.

So get creative! Try these activities. Find the opportunities in everyday living.

You are a teacher. Teach what you know best . . . the things you love.

Art for Art's Sake

Children love to express themselves through their art. It's a time when they can let their imaginations run free. Have you ever noticed the concentration and earnestness in their manner? Ten circus clowns doing back flips could file past, but marker will not leave paper until the fourth wheel on the alien's dune buggy is completed.

I think that's great. Especially when the finished project, whether it's a simple drawing or **MELTED CRAYON ART**, fills a child with so much pleasure. And for good reason:

He has a vision, and he made it happen.

It's part of a long tradition, isn't it?

MICHELANGELO UNDER A CHAIR gives children a sense of what it's like to create something that we still stand in awe of today. They can actually begin to feel like a famous artist did so very long ago!

SUNCATCHERS add such shimmering beauty to a room. On a glorious day they're not to be missed.

Kids love to create from nothing, or decorate the ordinary, and most of all they enjoy seeing their work displayed. In my house we have a special gallery wall with changing exhibits using **DOODLE GLASS PHOTO FRAMES**.

Our children's changing art is a sign of their growing interests, abilities, and maturity.

It's the bits and pieces of who they are.

And all of us feel so proud!

Lamp Light, Western Night... or Beaded Bright

I love lamp shades. For me, they harken back to a more romantic time. Especially when I walk into those specialized lamp shade stores and I see beautiful silk and pleated shades in lovely curving shapes that seem to have popped right out of a Victorian parlor. And all that fringe!!!

But there's something else about lamp shades that I like. Their inexpensive versatility. The simplest kind, once redesigned, can light up a room in more ways than one. This is great news for any child who wants to jazz up her room, or any teenager who's hankering for a more sophisticated space.

Western Nights

Here's a popular motif with the older set. It's laid back. It's muted in tone. And it's a perfect setting for a guitar . . . electric or otherwise.

HERE'S WHAT YOU'LL NEED:

Inexpensive standard white lamp shade, approximately 10 inches in diameter at the base (without pleats or plastic backing)

Large index card

X-acto knife

Double-sided tape

Sponge

Newspaper

Acrylic paints in earth tones such as deep blues, greens, oranges, or golds

Sewing needle large enough to thread ribbon or leather

Two yards ⅜"-wide grosgrain ribbon or leather cording

Beads and/or feathers

LET'S GET STARTED:

✺ Ask your kids to think of the shapes that remind them of a night on the plains. A moon may come to mind. Stars. Cactus. Snakes. A howling coyote. If you have a cookie cutter in the shape of a cactus, star, or half-moon, great. If not, draw their shapes (and any others) freehand on an index card. Cut around the outline of your drawing with the X-acto knife. Discard the cutout shapes.

🖐 Back your new stencil with two pieces of double-sided tape and attach it to the lamp shade.

🖐 Take a small piece of sponge and dab it into the paint. Blot several times on newspaper and then lightly dab the sponge on the space framed by your stencil. Then gently lift the stencil off the shade. Repeat this process on another part of the shade using another stencil design and, if you'd like, another color as well. Let the paint dry.

🖐 Thread the needle with the ribbon or leather and poke it through the shade approximately half an inch from the lower rim. Pull the ribbon/leather through, leaving about 10 extra inches dangling to be used later for tying a knot when the stitching is

complete. Sew a whipstitch (go in on the outside, wrap the ribbon/leather up and around the edge, and thread it back in again from the outside) around the lower rim of the shade, allowing about one inch between each stitch.

🖐 When you have completed stitching around the shade, remove the needle and tie the remaining ribbon to the dangling ribbon, adding beads and/or feathers between knots.

QUICK TIP: Try combining colors on individual stencils for a very textured, very earthy look.

For the coyote or any other shape you might find unusual, place a piece of tracing paper over a picture of the object and draw the outline. Then lay the paper over an index card and press down hard with a pencil as you copy over the outline. Lift the paper and, following the indentations, trace the shape with a pencil on to the card. Then cut the same as above.

Beaded Bright Lights

You can light up a desk, night table, dresser, or piano with this whimsical lamp shade. Place it near an open window, and it will seem to take on a life of its own!

HERE'S WHAT YOU'LL NEED:

Darning needle

Plain lamp shade of any size

Craft wire

Buttons, charms, beads

LET'S GET STARTED:

✋ Use the darning needle to poke holes around the bottom edge of the lamp shade, about one and a half inches apart.

✋ Twist one end of the wire to form a $1/8''$ loop. Slide a bead on the wire from the other end to reach the loop. Make another loop on top of the bead to hold in place. Leave a small space and make another loop. Add a bead and loop again.

✋ Or try it another way. String the beads by stacking them on top of each other. Or make a wire spiral by placing beads in between the twists.

✋ Loop the decorated wires through the holes in the shade, twisting to hold in place.

QUICK TIP: Don't forget the base. A lamp shade does not live on bulb alone! Bead a length of wire twice the height of the base and wind it around the base in a crisscrossed or random fashion.

IF YOUR KIDS GO HAYWIRE!

Give a child a "design concept," and sometimes she'll go wild!

"What else can I decorate!" she might exclaim. Well, she can stencil on wastepaper baskets, planters, and placemats. Also photo album covers, picture frames, doors, and ceilings! (What better way to lie back and look at the stars whenever the mood strikes?)

And if your kids are simply "wired" with beads, have them decorate window pull shades, the flip tops of fabric on board jewelry boxes, and window valances. Kids can keep going as long as buttons, beads, and other baubles last.

Sandpaper Art

← IRON ON MEDIUM

🖐 ← SANDPAPER DRAWING (FACE DOWN)

← WHITE DRAWING PAPER

Have you ever taken a close look at a pointillist painting? Every element in the painting is composed of dots. Thousands and thousands of dots that you can see up close but that blend into an image when you step back away from it. When visiting an exhibit of impressionism at an art gallery, my youngest son was fascinated. "Wow. That must have taken a long time. Look at those dots!" Well, I suppose it did. But here's a way to create a perfectly wonderful piece of pointillist art in seconds. What's the magic ingredient? A dot, you say? Uh-uh. *An iron!*

HERE'S WHAT YOU'LL NEED:

A few sheets of medium-grain sandpaper

Crayons (bright colors suggested)

White paper

Iron

Plenty of elbow grease!

LET'S GET STARTED:

🖐 Pick out an array of wonderfully bright crayons from the crayon bin. Bright blues, greens, purples, and reds are great.

🖐 Create a design on a sheet of sandpaper, pressing very hard as you color. Designs that use blocks of color rather than thin lines work best here. Again, *press hard* as you fill in the shapes with your crayons!

🖐 When you're done, turn the sandpaper over on top of a plain white piece of drawing paper.

🖐 An adult should heat up the iron on low temperature and then iron the back of the sandpaper as if ironing a hanky. Pass it over the back evenly and slowly two or three times.

🖐 Count to three, and slowly pick the sandpaper up off the paper. There it is. Sandpaper pointillism!

Never mind French impressionists. You'll have your own very "impressive" artist in residence!

If Your Young Child Says, "I Want to Iron Too!"

You might want to try letting him do so, but only with your hand on top of his. Kids do want to try grown-up tasks and have to begin to learn sometime. Still, the iron has to keep moving over the back of the sandpaper, and your youngster might decide to press down too long in one spot if he gets distracted! So keep him going by holding the iron together.

DEBBIE

Melted Crayon Art

Pointillism gives way to twentieth-century abstract.

Ask your older kids: "Wanna just slab the crayons anywhere?" They're bound to say yes. After all, it sounds like it's going to be a mess. How could they possibly resist that?!

HERE'S WHAT YOU'LL NEED:

Electric frying pan or warming tray

Aluminum foil

Crayon stubs with paper removed (fluorescent colors work beautifully)

Heavy paper or blank stationery cards

LET'S GET STARTED:

❦ Line the frying pan or warming tray with aluminum foil.

❦ Put it on low heat.

❦ Drop the little bits of crayon right onto the foil and watch them carefully as they begin to melt. Always keep the temperature low and keep an eye on the wax.

❦ When the crayons are completely melted, gently lay a piece of heavy paper or a stationery card over the melted wax.

❦ Lift it up. The colors should be brilliant . . . and spread everywhere in a fascinating abstract design. Let it cool and harden.

❦ Do this with a number of blank stationery cards and then wrap them all up with ribbon for a lovely, colorful gift.

QUICK TIP: Why not add your own personal stamp to the back of your designer cards? Take a stamp with the first letter of your name, add a little poster paint to an ink pad, and give the back of each card a unique signature. Artists always sign their work!

PAN COVERED WITH ALUMINUM FOIL

MELTED CRAYON BITS

LOW

LOW

Potato Gem Jewelry

Surely you've got a potato or two in your house that never did make it into the oven? It's soft. Wrinkled. Maybe it's even sprouted a bit? *Well, don't throw it out!* It's a gem.

HERE'S WHAT YOU'LL NEED:

For the potato beads:

Old potatoes

Potato peeler

Sharp knife

Wooden skewers

Oasis foam bricks (available from a florist)

Foam paintbrushes

Acrylic paints

For the necklace or bracelet:

String

Ribbon or elastic

Beads

If you're willing to put in a bit of prep work, the final stringing part of this activity is ideal for birthday parties. Kids love trading creative ideas as they design their own jewelry.

LET'S GET STARTED:

🖐 Peel one potato (enough for one necklace). This is a great job for your kids.

🖐 Cut it into small (half-inch or so) chunks. I usually start by cutting the potato in half.

🖐 Poke these chunks onto the wooden skewers. You'll want to help your younger ones so that they don't poke themselves. Also, do make sure the beads are well spaced so that there's room to paint them eventually on all sides while still skewered. Let the chunks dry. One of the easiest ways to do this is to poke the skewers standing into the foam bricks.

🖐 After about 24 hours, these little spud chunks are going to turn a funny gray-black color, which is fine. Twist them on the skewer once in a while as they dry. Wait until they get rock-hard. It will take about a week.

🖐 During this time you might want to take a book out of the library on stones and gems found around the world. Suggest to your

children that they pick a stone they'd most like to create. (I like turquoise, so that's what I'll describe here.)

🖐 Spread newspaper all around. Holding the bottom of each skewer like a handle, dip your foam brush into the turquoise-colored acrylic paint and begin painting your beads. There are so many little nooks and crannies on the potato that it actually does look like a stone!

🖐 After you're through with the turquoise, let dry. Then, dip another smaller foam brush into the black paint and give your bead a little detail so that it looks like the real thing.

🖐 Then take a bit of newspaper and rub it around in a few crevices so that the black smears slightly, creating a wonderfully weathered-looking bead! Let dry.

🖐 Finally, string your beads on ribbon or elastic, perhaps alternating with loose beads from another old necklace, to fashion an interesting pattern.

And you're done! You'll have a beautiful faux turquoise necklace that could fool anyone. Wearable food. Hmmm.

QUICK TIP: Maybe your kids would like to get real snazzy and use primary colors instead. I have a bracelet with potato beads of every color. People are always asking where I got it. I like to reply, "My kids made it! Out of old potatoes!"

Record Player Art

I still have my little record player from when I was a child. It's got polka dots on it. Remember all those Beatles albums? Whenever I look at my record player, "She Loves You" plays in my ears, over and over, round and round.

If you don't have your own player anymore, you could probably pick one up at a garage sale. I see them around here and there.

Then you'll be all set for record player plate art. First I'm going to describe how to do the basic plates, and then we'll move on to other projects you can put together once the plates are in hand.

All right! Let's go for a spin!

HERE'S WHAT YOU'LL NEED:

Old record player

Plain white paper plates

Markers

LET'S GET STARTED:

🖐 Poke a hole in the center of a paper plate. (I don't bother with a ruler. I just eyeball it.) Place it on the spindle.

🖐 Say to your kids, "What speed? 33, 45, or 78?" (I prefer 78 rpm.)

🖐 Turn on the record player, and while the plate is spinning, pick up a marker and very lightly place the tip toward the center of the plate. Then start moving your hand outward toward the rim. You will see a swirl of color begin to form.

🖐 While the same plate is still spinning, place another marker on a fresh spot and draw that color outward also. A lovely color combination of connecting circles will appear.

🖐 Take the plate off the spindle and replace it with another. This time move the marker so that it is heading toward the center of the plate. Something new is going to happen. You will end up with loop-de-loops! How did that happen?! It might make you a little dizzy, but the kids will think it's gorgeous! And really rather amazing.

🖐 Add another color to your loop plate, either using the same technique or the first one.

🖐 Finally, you can either arrange an assortment of these pieces of art on your wall or cut out a circle or square in the middle of one plate and tape a class picture to the back. Punch a hole in the top, hang your plate frame from a ribbon, and you've got a new, highly personalized wall decoration!

Bean Tambourine

This will make a terrific addition to your homemade musical instrument collection.

HERE'S WHAT YOU'LL NEED:

Two heavy-quality paper plates (with rims)

Old record player

Masking tape

Markers

Paper clips or clothespins

Hole puncher

Shoelaces or ribbons

Assorted beans and rice

LET'S GET STARTED:

Wait! Don't poke a hole in the center!

🤟 Place the plate upside down on the turntable and fasten it down along the edges with masking tape.

🤟 Pick up your markers and color as directed for RECORD PLAYER ART.

🤟 When you have completed two plates, place the rims together, design facing out, and hold them together using either paper clips or clothespins.

🤟 Punch out holes about an inch apart along the rims.

🤟 Go to your doo-dah basket and pull out colorful shoelaces or yarn. Begin sewing up your tambourine, leaving several inches dangling from the first hole. You can use a regular in-and-out stitch or a whipstitch.

🤟 When you have about three or four inches left, tell the kids it's noisemaker time! Pull out any containers of dried beans and rice you might have on hand and drop a handful inside the plates. Lentils make a softer sound. Rice, a light rainy sound. Kidney beans, a robust sound.

🤟 Finish sewing up your tambourine, make a knot with the ends, tie a bow, and let what's left dangle. You might want to add a few beads.

Then hand a pot to one person and a pan to another, give out a spoon or two, pick up your tambourine, and shake, rattle, and roll!

Spiraling Mobile

This can be a spectacular dazzler. Suddenly your plate art will transform into a cascade of swirl and twirl.

HERE'S WHAT YOU'LL NEED:

Record player art (made on several plain white plates)

Scissors

Ribbon

Beads

Embroidery hoop or metal hanger

Choose your window! This mobile will brighten any rainy day.

LET'S GET STARTED:

🖐 Following the circles around a plate, cut in a spiraling direction, moving inward as you cut.

🖐 Just before you make it to the center, stop. Tie a knot at one end of the ribbon, add a bead, and then just slip the other end of the ribbon through the hole until the plate (what's left of it!) is resting on the bead.

🖐 Tie the other end of the ribbon to a brightly painted embroidery hoop or a hanger that you've bent into a circle.

🖐 Do the same with several plates. When you lift up the embroidery hoop, you'll see an astonishing spiraling mobile.

QUICK TIP: You might also want to hang from the embroidery hoop several inches of beaded ribbon between the plates. It'll give the mobile an even more intricate and festive look.

Ribbons, beads, bows, and spirals. Sounds like a celebration to me!

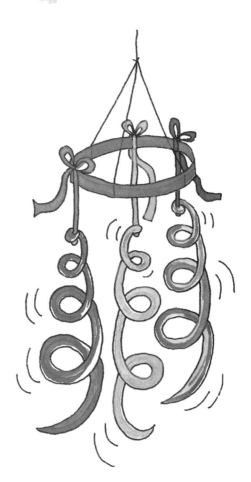

Doodle Glass Photo Frames

Ever notice that foggy windows and kids' fingers are never very far apart? Suddenly you see hearts and names and the sun and mice? Well, that's because it's fun to draw on glass.

Finally, here's a chance for school-age kids to make it stick! Changes in weather won't melt it away, your kids can use many different colors, and in the end they'll have a very inventive frame for a favorite photo.

Hang it on the wall and watch them catch a glimpse of themselves and their artwork at the exact same time!

HERE'S WHAT YOU'LL NEED:

Inexpensive glass frames with clips

Permanent markers

Acrylic paints and paintbrushes, or paint pens (available at stationery stores)

Construction paper

Photos

Explain to your kids that photos don't always tell the whole story. Sometimes they need help. A doodle or two can work with the photo to truly describe the moment.

LET'S GET STARTED:

👋 Unclip the glass frame and wipe it down carefully with window cleaner.

👋 Figure out where you'd like to place the photo (which, by the way, should always be considerably smaller than the frame). Smack in the middle is fine. Sometimes off center looks great. A slight tilt will give this project a very playful look. Anything goes!

👋 Once you've placed the photo, outline the photo's position on the back side of the glass with a marker, using either a ruler as a guide or a free-form squiggle line.

👋 Remove the photo and consider the space that's left. Outline the designs on the back side of the glass in black permanent marker or another dark color and then fill them in with paint pens (permanent) or acrylic paints. Remember that the pictures will be in reverse when the glass frame is put back together, and any words will have to be written backwards. The idea is to further illustrate the story the photo only begins to tell. (My son, for example, framed a photo of himself triumphantly holding a big fish he'd just caught. So he drew in a lake and a sun and fish jumping this way and that to show it had been a bright day and a big challenge to make that catch!)

🖐 Other ideas? If it's a new baby, you might want to draw in a bottle and bibs. If it's back to school, try a notebook and pencil and a September calendar. Encourage your kids to consider the moment in context, "What else was going on just then?" and let them conjure up a memory.

🖐 While their artwork is drying, have the kids choose a piece of colored paper on which to mount their photos.

🖐 Have them use the backing of the frame as a kind of stencil by laying it on the paper and outlining the shape lightly in pencil on the paper. Then cut it out.

🖐 Affix the photo to the paper, place it against the glass, clip on the back of the frame, and you have a wonderful "picture story" to hang on the wall.

QUICK TIP: It's not a great idea for preschoolers to handle glass, since there are too many chances for dropping and breaking. Instead, have them do all their doodling directly on the paper, including the squiggle line frame shape. Then frame it and hang it. They'll be totally thrilled!

If Your Kids Want a Practice Run Before They Paint

Some kids might want to do a blueprint first on a sketch pad before painting permanently on glass. They might want to practice drawing a kayak, or skis, or a doll house. But if a line goes astray on the glass, just turn it into an added detail. Add a few more lines and you have ripples of water complementing your swan. Or a squiggle next to the basketball could be part of the net if you just add a few crisscross markings.

Apple Cinnamon Clay

Warm applesauce with a sprinkling of cinnamon on a crisp fall day. Doesn't that sound cozy? Well, now, let's adjust the recipe. Let's mix together equal parts applesauce and cinnamon.

Still sound delicious?

Probably not.

But guess what? It is still a great recipe. You can't eat it. But you can smell it. And you can mold it. And you can wear it.

Welcome to APPLE CINNAMON CLAY!

HERE'S WHAT YOU'LL NEED:

For the clay:

Commercial applesauce (homemade is too runny)

Ground cinnamon

For the charms:

Waxed paper

Rolling pin

Cookie cutters and other templates

Drinking straw

For the decorating details:

Toothpicks

Squeeze-bottle paints

Glue

Pin clasps

Plastic thread or elastic

LET'S GET STARTED:

Put away the eggs, the flour, the butter! This is an aromatic dough that requires but two ingredients—in very odd proportion!

❧ Mix together equal parts applesauce and cinnamon. I start with half a cup each for a small batch. It will look like kids' play clay very quickly. If it gets a little too sticky, add a bit more cinnamon. If it's too stiff, try a touch more applesauce.

❧ Scoop the mixture onto a piece of waxed paper, place another sheet of waxed paper on top, and roll it out until it's in a sheet about a quarter-inch thick.

❧ Stop and decide what "charms" you would like to create for jewelry. Stars, hearts, letters, cars, flowers, or really anything will work!

❧ Collect the cookie cutters you have about the house or make your own templates. You can make one by cutting out a piece of cardboard from a cereal box in whatever shape you'd like. Place it on top of the clay and simply trim away the dough from around the edges.

AUTUMN'S BEST APPLE SAUCE

ground cinnamon ECONOMY SIZE!

✋ Use the end of a drinking straw to poke a hole in the dough for threading the charms onto plastic thread or elastic.

✋ You might want to take a toothpick and carve out little details such as scales on a fish or a smile on a crescent moon.

✋ When your charms are all made, place them on a cooling rack and allow them to air-dry. It takes about 24 hours for them to become nice and hard.

✋ Time to decorate! Using squeeze-bottle paints, create a pattern of any kind on your charms and allow them to air-dry for a couple of hours.

✋ Fashion a pin by gluing a clasp on the back of your charm or a necklace by stringing together a few alphabet letter shapes or smaller charms.

These creations make great little gifts at school fairs. Take a piece of dark velveteen, frame it, and stick in an assortment of **apple cinnamon clay pins** for a tantalizing display!

QUICK TIP: If you'd like some sparkling charms, try adding glitter into the applesauce and cinnamon mix. Once it dries, every piece will shine bright! Added to the ribbon that decorates a gift, it will be like giving your friend two presents instead of one.

Suncatchers

When the sun streams through a stained-glass window, colors seem suspended, glistening in the air.
We expect to see such beauty mostly in places of worship or old historic homes.

But let's change that! You can create beautiful stained-glass windows for your home. And you don't need fancy bits of glass. Not even one piece. In fact, what you do need is something rather simple.

Grated crayon bits.

Yes, with a little creativity, a cheese grater, and waxed paper, you can devise elegant stained-glass windows that, just like the ones in hilltop cathedrals in France, are a joy to behold.

HERE'S WHAT YOU'LL NEED:

Crayons in assorted colors

Newspaper

Waxed paper

Cheese grater

Iron

Cloth napkin or handkerchief

Scissors

Black construction paper

Paper plates

Glue

Ribbon or fishing line

Find stray crayons around the house! Look under the curtains, behind the cushions, beneath the radiators!

LET'S GET STARTED:

✋ Unwrap the crayons. After peeling off the paper, sort them by colors. The blues here. The greens there. Purples to the right, yellows and oranges to the left.

✋ Spread out a bunch of newspaper or construction paper on a counter and then lay a piece of waxed paper on top.

✋ Now it's time to grate up those crayons. I like the cheese graters in the shape of cylinders: you twist the top back and forth, and the "cheese" (crayon) comes out the bottom.

←— WARM IRON

←— LINEN NAPKIN OR HANDKERCHIEF

←— WAXED PAPER

←— GRATED CRAYON ON WAXED PAPER

←— NEWSPAPER

🖐 Watch as the little bits of crayon sprinkle onto the waxed paper. If you would like, say, more blue toward the right side, just add some to the grater.

🖐 The colors will seem to fall into their own delicate pattern. When you're satisfied with the array of color, it's time for the next step.

🖐 Take another sheet of waxed paper and put it on top of the grated crayons.

🖐 Lay an old linen napkin or handkerchief on top of that.

🖐 This step is for an adult to handle. With an iron set on a warm temperature, press very slowly along the napkin, stopping and starting. The crayon will melt almost instantly. When you're done, pick up the napkin and take a peek. It's beautiful!

🖐 Center a paper plate over the "stained-glass window," using it as a template. Cut out a circle "pane of glass."

🖐 To create the lead on the stained-glass window, use the plate to cut a circle out of black construction paper. Then cut into the circle and begin cutting about a half-inch border. But don't cut too evenly! Real lead rarely looks perfect. It has soft swervy edges.

🖐 Cut out another couple of circles from the black construction paper disk, also making soft edges. These circles can be a bit narrower—$1/4''$ to $1/3''$ wide is fine.

🖐 Place the biggest circle around the edge of your stained glass, as a frame. Then take a smaller one or two and place them inside the others, again, over the stained glass.

🖐 Glue the circles down.

🖐 Cut little spokes out of either the center of your circle of black construction paper or a separate piece. Lay them down in a random fashion between the circles and over the stained glass to create the illusion of pieces of glass fitted together. Glue them down.

🖐 Punch a hole at the top of your stained-glass window and string some ribbon through the "lead."

🖐 Affix a hook over your window and hang up your own beautiful one-of-a-kind stained-glass window!

Watch the sun stream through and light up your own "historic" home. It does have history after all. Yours!

If Your Child Says, "Mine Isn't So Bright"

He might have chosen darker purples, greens, and blues. Explain that stained-glass windows come in all shapes, sizes, and colors, and that his is lovely. Maybe even show him pictures in books. Then pull out all the *neon* colors you can find from the crayon basket and say, "Here! Now let's try one that's already started shining!" He'll no doubt be thrilled with the results.

Salad Spin Art

When your salad spinner gets old and dingy, you might decide it's time for a new one . . . but don't throw the old one out! Salad spinners make terrific—surprise—painting gadgets.
Let me take you for a spin!

HERE'S WHAT YOU'LL NEED:

Salad spinner

Paper plates (white or solid-colored) cut to fit the bottom of the spinner

Index cards

Clay, plaster tack, or double-sided tape

Assortment of acrylic or poster paints in squeeze bottles

Glitter (optional)

Who would have thought that something as mundane as a salad spinner could create wonderful art? Well, you're about to find out.

LET'S GET STARTED:

✤ Take the lid off the salad spinner and affix the plate or index card with a piece of clay, plaster tack, or double-sided tape to the little nodule at the bottom of the spinner to hold it in place.

✤ Pick your paints. Bright colors give the finished product a lot of "snap."

✤ Drop the paint near the center of the plate. Add a few puddles here. A line of paint there. A few tiny dots all around. Feel free to use several colors.

✤ Pop the top of the spinner back on and give that crank a whirl! Spin it around for five to ten seconds, let it wind down, and then take the top off. If you wish, add some more paint and a pinch of glitter, then spin again.

👋 Remove the plate and let it dry. Then hang it on your wall or fridge—a few pieces will make a big splash!

It's so much fun to see the explosion of color! No matter what, the results are always a surprise.

QUICK TIPS: To make a **napkin ring**, take the painted paper plate and trim off the edge in a curvy shape. Then cut a round hole the size of a quarter in the center. Squeeze a napkin through, and you'll have a wonderful napkin ring, a bright addition to any party place setting.

To make a **gift card**, take a painted index card, fold it in half, punch a hole in one corner, and tie some ribbon through the hole. This makes a dazzling gift card for any present!

For a personalized **postcard**, use a postal regulation-sized card, spin some paint, jot a note, and send it off to Grandma!

You can also create a **frame**. Cut out a rectangle in the middle of the plate, slightly smaller than your picture. Then glue the picture to the back of the plate and hang it on the wall (use some ribbon too, if you like).

GRAMPA, HAVE A COLORFUL DAY!

Michelangelo Under a Chair

Talk to your children about Michelangelo and how it took him years (1508–12) to paint the ceiling of the Sistine Chapel in the Vatican in Rome. Explain how he would lie on his back on a scaffold, facing the ceiling, and paint and paint and paint. In dim light. In the heat. In the cold.

Then pull over a wooden picnic chair or kitchen chair and say, "Artists, it's your turn!"

HERE'S WHAT YOU'LL NEED:

Large sheets of drawing paper

Wooden picnic chairs or kitchen chairs

Markers, pencils, acrylic paints, and brushes

Inspire your kids to consider art from an entirely new vantage point!

LET'S GET STARTED:

✤ Tape the paper to the bottom side of each chair.

✤ Wiggle under (one to a chair, of course) and place a basket of pencils and markers within reach.

✤ Now go ahead and create a masterpiece.

The kids will no doubt be enthralled. Somehow there's a real intimacy between the art and the creator that doesn't quite happen out in the open with a desk and chair.

Try it. You'll see!

QUICK TIP: If your kids want to use paints, push out from under the chair for a moment and carefully wipe their brush off at the side of the paint container before they start painting the "ceiling." Otherwise, they may be painting their heads!

IF YOUR CHILD SAYS, "I'M UNCOMFORTABLE UNDER HERE"

Some kids may be uneasy in what they perceive to be a small space. Put a piece of paper under a picnic table or kitchen table instead, and if his arms can't quite stretch while he's lying on his back, then let him sit, look up, and draw that way. Tell him Michelangelo used all manner of positions to get the job done!

Dream It, Create It, Use It!

Whether we're children or adults, we all like to feel useful. It leaves a person with a sense of purpose and fulfillment.

Certainly creating things that others can admire has its own special usefulness. Enjoying beautiful things feeds the soul.

In this section we're going to create things that the whole family can use in a more practical way. Things that will help you through the day. Things that make responsibilities easier to remember (PING-PONG BALL PERPETUAL CALENDAR), nights brighter (BEESWAX CANDLES), family mementos more visible (FUNKY FRAMES), and quick desserts even more of a kick (SOLAR OVEN TREATS).

I know the joy my children have always derived from the things we've created for our family's use, whatever the object. And we all gain a tremendous amount of satisfaction from making something together as a family. It's here. We're using it. What fun we had.

Handmade Gift Wrap

G ift wrap costs a lot of money. And when you have your children's birthdays, their friends' birthdays, holiday presents, and special family anniversaries, chances are you run out of paper quickly. Here's a way to always have some on hand . . . and to create a gift that easily stands out from the pile!

HERE'S WHAT YOU'LL NEED:

Big paper grocery bags or a roll of brown packing paper

Scissors

Newspaper

Slightly less than fresh apples, mushrooms, and green peppers

Knife

Forks

Paper towels

Acrylic paints

Paintbrushes

Ribbon, dried flowers, or colored pipe cleaners (optional)

LET'S GET STARTED:

🖐 Pull out those big paper bags you've been saving from the grocery store and cut them open along the sides and base to make flat sheets. Lay two or three pieces down side by side (be sure the unprinted sides are face up) over some newspaper and smooth with your hands.

🖐 Slice an apple in half along the stem.

🖐 Dry the freshly cut halves with paper toweling.

🖐 Stick a fork into the uncut side to create a handle for your stamp.

🖐 Choose a color and paint the cut side of the fruit. Not too heavily. Just enough to cover the surface evenly. It doesn't matter if the seeds are still there. It will only make for an even more interesting design.

🖐 Turn to the paper . . . and *stamp!* And then *stamp again.* Do it in rows. Do it in diagonals. Do it any which way.

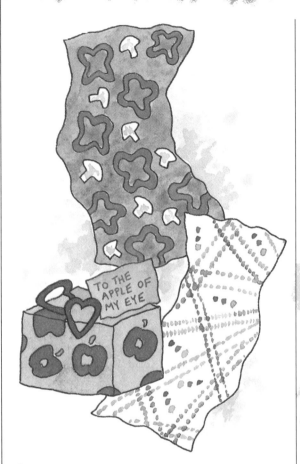

🖐 Slice the mushrooms in half. Depending on their size, use your fingers as a "handle" instead of a fork. But again, paint the cut sides of the vegetable and then, on another sheet of paper, press, press, press! You can squish it a little from side to side too. So many interesting shapes and patterns suddenly happen!

🖐 When your paper is dry, use it to wrap a present. You might accent with bright ribbon and a few decorative details like dried flowers, or pipe cleaners bent into heart, shamrock, or star shapes.

QUICK TIP: Need some extra holiday paper? Pull out some festive color paints. A pepper with three or four nodules, stamped in green paint, will make lovely shamrocks! Try slicing a potato in half and carving out a pumpkin outline. Paint on orange or black and start stamping for a Halloween wrap, treat bags, or wall hanging!

IF YOUR YOUNG ONE SAYS, "I WANT TO MAKE MORE!"

You might reply, "Okay! Let's paint with wheels!" Ask him to dip into his collection of little cars. Show him how to roll the wheels in some paint (put a little color on a plate), give him a practice run on newspaper, then point him toward the paper. Exclaim, "Go ahead! Let it roll!" He'll love this **traffic wrap.** For added effect, try randomly dotting vertical rows of red, yellow, and green dots. Wrapping paper on a fast track, I think. Rinse off the paint from the wheels when you're finished.

🖐 For a little stem finesse, try dabbing a brush in some green paint and adding a dash of color at the top center of your apple print.

🖐 Hang your paper up to dry on an indoor clothes line, draping it over the line or clipping it with laundry clips.

🖐 Cut a green pepper in half crosswise. Again, dry the freshly cut area on each half with paper toweling. Then paint the cut part of the vegetable with white paint. Press it firmly on the dried apple print paper once, twice, three times. Watch as a flurry of early snowflakes cascades over the apple prints! Hang the paper up to dry.

Stained-Glass Votive Candle Holders

I've noticed a pattern. My juice glasses start to look grungy six months after I buy them. I think this must be true for lots of people because whenever I visit a garage sale there's always a bunch of juice glasses on display. Maybe it's because they've been in a dishwasher thousands of times? The good news is that while they might have lost their luster as glasses, they've only just begun to live as votive candle holders!

HERE'S WHAT YOU'LL NEED:

Tissue paper

Lackluster standard juice glasses

Scissors

Household glue

Small bowl

Paintbrush

Pressed dried flowers (optional)

Take a peek in old gift boxes and bags and start collecting brightly colored tissue paper. Even the patterned kind will work nicely. When you've got a nice array, line up your glasses and begin.

(Try this activity in the morning so the candle holders are ready to glow at dinnertime.)

LET'S GET STARTED:

❦ Cut the sheets of tissue paper into little squares, triangles, circles, diamonds, and rectangles. Older kids might want to try heart, fish, star, and flower shapes as well.

❦ Squeeze white household glue in a small bowl and dilute with a few drops of water to create a milkshake-like consistency.

❦ Brush a light coat of the glue mixture on the outside of a glass.

❦ In an overlapping pattern, begin applying the shapes to the glass, lightly smoothing each piece out with your fingers as you go along. Rest any larger detailed shapes on top of the paper pieces with a touch of extra glue, or . . .

❦ Glue some pressed flowers between the glass and the paper, or . . .

❦ Simply take a (pre-measured) strip of patterned tissue paper and wrap it around the glass in one swoop.

JUST GLU IT WHITE GLUE

QUICK TIP: When working with young children, you might want to apply glue to the glass a section at a time, so fingers don't get too gooey to handle the paper.

SAFETY NOTE:

An adult should always be present when burning candles.

🖐 When the outside of the glass is covered, you can finish it off with a coating or two of glue and water. It will drip all over a bit, but that's fine. By the way, at this point your candle holder might not look too alluring! Just wait until it dries!

🖐 After about eight hours, your candle holder will be set for service. Place a little candle inside, light it, and watch the dull juice glass turned candle holder shimmer with a new stained-glass life.

Ice Candles

This is one of those activities I love because it sounds so impossible, so mysterious, and so beautiful. . . . It's Fire and Ice! "What is that?" your kids might ask. "It's one cool candle!"

MELT PARAFFIN IN COFFEE CAN

← SAUCEPAN WITH A FEW INCHES OF WATER

HERE'S WHAT YOU'LL NEED:

Saucepan

Coffee can

Paraffin and candle stubs

Candle coloring

Heavy-duty one-gallon plastic bag

Ice

Hammer

Tall taper candle

Empty one-quart paper milk container

LET'S GET STARTED:

🐾 An adult should fill the bottom of the saucepan with a few inches of water and place a coffee can in the center to create a double boiler. Place a chunk of paraffin inside the can, along with whatever extra pieces of candle stubs you might have around the house, to begin the "designer color" process. If you'd like, add a little candle coloring. You don't need much. A teaspoon will do. Stir occasionally, keeping a constant eye on the wax. It is flammable.

🐾 While this is going on, your child can fill the gallon plastic bag about three-quarters of the way full with ice. Secure the top. Use a hammer to break the ice into small chunks (but not too small).

🐾 While the wax is still melting down and taking on wonderful color, think "wick." Here's an easy trick. Your school-age child can place the slender taper candle into the middle of the milk container and pack the ice around it. (For smaller containers, just use the remains of whatever half-used candle you have hanging around the house.)

FILL WITH ICE CHUNKS

TAPER CANDLE

DAIRY D-LITE MILK ONE QUART

BOSSY SAYS: MOO!

🖐 Continue giving the wax a few stirs as it melts. When it's done, using pot holders, an adult can lift the can out of the saucepan and pour the wax directly into the milk carton over the ice and around the candle. Make sure the wick is standing tall. You'll hear crackling and popping.

🖐 After a few minutes you'll need to drain off the water. You might need to do this a couple of times.

🖐 Let the wax harden completely.

🖐 Peel off the milk carton. (Use scissors if necessary to get started.)

Depending on the color of the candle and the ambiance of the room, your candle will look like a colorful swirl of Swiss cheese or an ancient piece of marble.

QUICK TIPS: Who can wait? Yes, some kids enjoy the anticipation of waiting for the candle to harden in its own time. Others just can't take the "heat." If you want the candle to set by a faster clock, run the outside of the container under cool tap water.

To display the candle, stand it on a plate or in a small ceramic container and surround it with marbles.

IF YOUR YOUNGEST SAYS, "HEY, WHAT CAN I DO?!"

Well, it's true, since this activity involves the stove and a real hammer, younger children should be supervised carefully. Send her on a "candle treasure hunt" to locate usable stubs. Let her help fill the milk carton with ice using a cup measuring spoon, or gently strip the carton from the candle. She can also be the one to select the marbles that encircle the candle when it is placed on a plate. Finally, give her the job of saying "Ta-da!" as you light the candle and everyone stands round proudly watching their creation flicker in the moonlight.

SAFETY NOTE:

An adult should always be present when burning candles.

Funky Frames

So many fabulous photographs. So few frames . . .

But not anymore!

Kids can make and decorate their own dynamic frames for their favorite pictures and display them in their bedrooms or give them to friends. For the basic frames, all they need are empty cereal boxes. Any kind.

Look for all those photos that are on the brink of getting bent, torn, or lost! They're going to have their own unique home.

Pasta Pix

HERE'S WHAT YOU'LL NEED:

Empty cereal boxes

Household glue

Pasta shells, elbows, rotini, wheels

Photos

LET'S GET STARTED:

❀ Cut out one side of the cereal box.

❀ Fold the cardboard in half and then fold it one more time in the other direction.

❀ Draw a little rectangle in the thickest corner. An adult, using a sharp pair of scissors, should cut out the shape.

❀ Unfold the cardboard and . . . ta-da! You have a surprise frame. It's time for the kids to decorate it.

❀ Put a few small globs of glue on the plain gray side of the frame and start affixing pieces of pasta. Any shape. All kinds of noodles. Then put a few more globs down. Add more pasta. Fill the entire frame. Let dry.

❀ Finally, attach your photo inside the frame.

❀ Sit back and enjoy the picture!

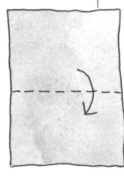

← FOLD

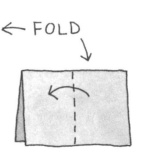

CUT

QUICK TIP: Take the frame outside and ask an adult to spray it all over with some bright silver paint. It's a very jazzy look.

Junk Frames

What about those photos that are really wild? You know. The ones where the kids are wearing wacky sunglasses and chasing each other around the tree.

Well, those photos deserve to be framed too!

Yes. They deserve to be surrounded by junk!

HERE'S WHAT YOU'LL NEED:

Old junk drawer to rummage through

Household glue

Old scratched-up box frames or garage sale frames with wide borders

Approach that drawer in your house . . . you know . . . the one you occasionally empty in an unsuccessful attempt to clean it all out and so everything goes back in! It's overflowing with little bits of stuff like pieces from your kids' toys, buttons, gum wrappers, old plastic haircurlers, pen tops, broken combs, old keys, and stray paper clips.

Well . . . open it up and dig in!

LET'S GET STARTED:

🖐 Take out an assortment of junk. The odder the shape the better.

🖐 Again, put little globs of glue on your frame and affix whatever funny little item strikes your fancy.

🖐 Take the particularly funky photo you like to the photocopying store and get it enlarged in color. Put it in place, and you'll find yourself with the perfect theme frame for your goofiest pictures.

QUICK TIPS: When it's dry, take your frame outside and have an adult spray-paint your junk creation in bright, bright gold paint. Who says junk isn't worth its weight in gold?

Do you have a dog? Well, take a scratched-up plastic box frame and glue dog biscuits around the border. Then frame a picture of your canine buddy! But do make sure you hang this tempting frame high on the wall. Otherwise, in the morning you may just find it on the floor, quite well chewed.

Beeswax Candles

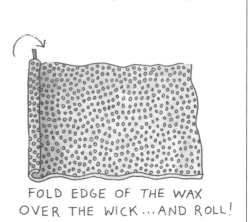

FOLD EDGE OF THE WAX
OVER THE WICK...AND ROLL!

This is a safe and easy way to make candles with your children. The tasks are simple. Cutting, pressing, and rolling! Even little ones will be thrilled. It requires no melting other than that provided by your warm breath. And kids can have a great time choosing and combining colors, especially for the fancier version.

Are your kids impatient? If they are, this activity is perfect for them.

The Little Candle That Could

HERE'S WHAT YOU'LL NEED:

Sheets of beeswax in a variety of colors

Ruler

Wicks

Scissors

Small decorated terra-cotta pots

Sand

You'll want to take a quick trip to the local craft store to pick up an assortment of beeswax sheets in different colors along with some wicks.

LET'S GET STARTED:

❧ Lay a ruler or yardstick right down the middle of a sheet of beeswax. Press the edge into the sheet to make a neat indentation down the center.

❧ Cut the sheets in half.

❧ Take a piece of wicking and lay it on the edge of your half-sheet (along the shorter side), about a quarter-inch in from the edge. Trim the length of wick so that it's about half an inch longer than the wax.

❧ Press that quarter-inch of wax securely over the wick to hold it nice and snug. Here's where you might add a little warm breath! It really will soften the wax.

❧ Roll the wax over and over down to the end until it blossoms into a candle. Done!

❧ Hold the candle upright and push the end opposite the wick lightly down on the table to flatten the base.

❧ Pour a little sand into a small decorated terra-cotta pot. Settle the candle in the pot and then add a bit more sand to further support your beautiful creation.

Your children's faces will "light up" with delight . . . right along with the candles at dinnertime!

Spiral Roll Candles

Challenging for the more advanced skills of your older kids, this technique makes a unique design.

HERE'S WHAT YOU'LL NEED:

Sheets of beeswax in a variety of colors

Ruler

Scissors

Wicks

LET'S GET STARTED:

🖐 This time place the edge of the ruler on the diagonal of a sheet of wax. Press down firmly. Then cut the wax along the indentation into two triangular pieces.

🖐 Snip off a bit of the top end.

🖐 Place the wick along the vertical side—

again, about a quarter-inch from the edge—and press the excess wax over it.

🖐 Now for the beautiful twist. Choose one of the other colored sheets and cut a strip that's about half an inch wide and the same length as the diagonal of the first sheet.

🖐 Press that strip along the length of the diagonal, overlapping the pieces a bit about a quarter of an inch.

🖐 Now start rolling in from the vertical end. Do you see what happens? Spirals!

🖐 Make another candle beginning with the other half of the first sheet, and you have a pair of candles for a perfect gift!

HANDMADE CANDLES FROM ONE OF YOUR BRIGHT STUDENTS!

QUICK TIP: Little ones might also enjoy using cookie cutters for **whimsically shaped candles!** Have them select a cookie cutter and press down very firmly to create six identical shapes on the wax sheets. Pop the shapes out. Sort the shapes into two equal piles. Center a wick on top of the first pile with half an inch extending over the edge. Press it down, and then neatly stack the other three shapes on top of the wick. Press firmly to hold the stack together. Set the chunky candle upright. Voilà! A candle to warm your heart!

SAFETY NOTE:

An adult should always be present when burning candles.

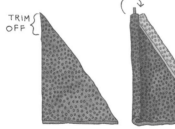

TRIM OFF

FOLD WAX OVER WICK, ADD STRIP OF DIFFERENT COLORED WAX, AND ROLL!

Bedtime Buddies

Just when it seems your child has drifted off to sleep for the night, a plaintive voice echoes through the hallway, "Mom! I can't sleep! I think there's a monster in my closet!"

So you check the closet carefully. "Nope, honey. No monsters." But it doesn't help much.

Well, here's a very special nightlight that will help your child conduct his very own "monster patrol." He can even switch it on and off without leaving his bed!

HERE'S WHAT YOU'LL NEED:

Scissors

Lunch bags or decorator gift bags

Glue

Yarn, pipe cleaners, charms, ribbons, glitter, beads, felt

Plastic lightweight flashlights

Rubber bands

An angel? Ladybug? Goofy alien? First decide who's manning the monster patrol!

LET'S GET STARTED:

👋 Cut out little holes for eyes, a nose, and a mouth in the side of the bag.

👋 Glue on ribbon eyebrows and a charm nose or stick in pipe-cleaner antennae. Glue some glitter on his cheeks or outline her mouth in shiny beads. And don't forget hair!

Glue on some braided yarn and fashion a major "do."

👋 When the bag is finished, slip it over the top of the flashlight with a rubber band, just above the switch.

Your very own monster patrol. He's on and off duty when you say so!

QUICK TIP: A particularly scared young child might need a sweet nightlight persona. A bunny with felt ears that stick out at funny angles, and no cutouts on the bag, will give forth a comforting, ultrasoft (and fuzzy) light.

Ping-Pong Ball Perpetual Calendar

Keeping track of each other's hectic schedule is a challenge for everyone in the family.

A fun way to make sure no important appointments or responsibilities get lost in the shuffle is to gather together all of your old ping-pong balls, open your daily calendar, and serve.

Well, not quite.

HERE'S WHAT YOU'LL NEED:

Ruler

Markers

Foam cork or tagboard

Adhesive-backed Velcro

Lots of ping-pong balls (or plastic milk caps; see Quick Tip)

Markers

Charms

Four magnets

This is a great opportunity, while you're creating the grid, to talk with little children about the number of days in a week, in a month, in a year, and even how February 29 leaps into the picture!

LET'S GET STARTED:

❦ Using a ruler and marker, divide up the board into seven days across the top. Then measure out five rows of boxes along the vertical side.

❦ Cut the Velcro strips into 31 sets of corresponding pieces, and press them one at a time into each of the boxes. (If you can't find the self-sticking kind, you can use regular Velcro and glue.)

❦ Put the corresponding piece of Velcro on one side of 31 ping-pong balls.

❦ Write a big number for each day of the month right onto the ping-pong ball. Use different colors or write the numbers in block print or fancy swirls. After all, each day is usually very different from the next!

❦ Cut 12 rectangular tags to affix to the top of the calendar. These will each bear the name of a different month. Discuss with your kids what special things each month brings to mind and encourage them to have fun illustrating their thoughts. The word "December" might be surrounded by fir trees. "April" may sport a couple of umbrellas! And "July" a super-bright sun. Or your child may prefer to draw a big birthday cake for "July" since that's her birthday month. Put Velcro on the back of each tag and, of course, at the top of your chart.

❦ Pull together the remaining ping-pong balls. These may be decorated in very particular ways. Do your kids play soccer, baseball, or basketball? Just create the sport's tell-tale ball pattern on one of the ping-pong

off! Riiiiiiippppppppp!!!!! Another successful month has gone by, and the kids get to set the whole thing up all over again.

Uh-oh. The big science project is due the first week of May!

Well, you can always draw a test tube on a ball . . . or attach a little eye dropper to the board.

A ping-pong ball calendar definitely makes it entertaining to stay on top of what's happening!

QUICK TIP: If you don't have ping-pong balls, use plastic caps from milk containers instead. Put Velcro on one side and either cut little pieces of paper and glue them on the inside of the caps or buy little adhesive dots in the local stationery store and stick them to the inside. Then write in the numbers and fasten them to the board.

If Your Children Say, "Hey, What Should We Do? Christie's Book Report Is on the Same Day as My Class Play!"

"No problem," you say.

They can divide a ping-pong ball in half with a line. On one side of the line draw a little book. On the other side of the line draw an image that signifies the dramatic role. "There," you may say as they stick it on the board. "There's lots of room in a day for everything."

balls and place it on the day of the big game. Maybe you need to bring the dog to the vet? Draw a dog biscuit on one of the balls. Then there are those dentist appointments. Draw a giant tooth or a big toothy smile. Or . . .

❦ . . . this is where the charms come in. Instead of using a ping-pong ball, maybe you have a mini–soccer ball from a key chain. Put Velcro on that and add it to the appropriate day. Little empty dental floss containers fit perfectly on this calendar and are a clever reminder of dentist appointments. Do your kids want to squeeze in one more afternoon of fishing? Use a little stray rubber or plastic toy fish in your kids' toy containers. And you can always put a real little dog treat on the day "Simon" is due for his shots. Make sure you hang your calendar out of paw's reach!

❦ Glue the magnets to the back of the calendar and hang it on the refrigerator.

❦ At the end of the month comes a very satisfying moment. Pull those ping-pong balls

Solar Oven Treats

PLACE
SNACK
WAY
BACK

"**W**ow. I could fry an egg on the sidewalk it's so hot." Ever say that? I hear some people have actually done it! The summer can get awfully hot, so it's the perfect time to teach your kids how to crank up the heat by harnessing the sun in their own solar oven and cooking up quite a treat for themselves. (I'm not talking fried eggs, either!)

HERE'S WHAT YOU'LL NEED:

Sheet of black tagboard

Aluminum foil

Stapler

Apples, honey, raisins

Wait for a nice, hot sunny day!

LET'S GET STARTED:

✋ Lay the black tagboard down flat on a tabletop and cover one side completely with aluminum foil. (You can glue it in place or use a stapler.)

✋ Roll the tagboard in a diagonal direction, starting from one side, into a cone shape.

✋ Loosen up the shape a bit so that one side is really quite wide open and the other is small. Staple the small side flat and shut. You now have yourself a solar oven!

✋ Time to choose a treat. My kids' favorite is apples, honey, and raisins. Slice up a peeled apple and place the pieces in a small clear dish along with raisins and a little honey.

✋ Take the solar oven outside and position it so that the sun's rays are aimed right inside. Tuck the snack way back and cook this yummy apple concoction for 15–20 minutes.

✋ When the time is up, slip the treat out. But be careful! You might want to use an oven mitt. Solar energy can be hot stuff!

QUICK TIP: For an extra special treat, try a dollop of vanilla ice cream or frozen yogurt right on top. It's solar apples à la mode! By the way, pears peaches work nicely too.

Bookmarks

Kids love to read about things that capture their interests. Baseball, rain forests, dinosaurs. There are all kinds of books on these subjects available in the library. Fiction and nonfiction.

But relishing a triceratops doesn't have to stop with the book itself. Designing big elaborate bookmarks to keep track of their reading progress or to underline hot topics can bring hours of fun and become real page turners.

HERE'S WHAT YOU'LL NEED:

Tagboard

Pictures clipped from magazines, or drawings

Glue

Markers

Clear adhesive-backed plastic

This is an inspiring "after library" activity. When it's done, kids are rarin' to plunge right in.

LET'S GET STARTED:

❧ Cut a strip of tagboard about 12 inches by 4 inches.

❧ Have your kids draw pictures that reflect the themes of the books they've chosen and then cut them out. They might also want to flip through some magazines and cut out some illustrative photos.

❧ Glue the images onto the bookmark and create some decorative detail borders with markers.

❧ Cover the front of the bookmark with the clear adhesive-backed plastic to preserve the design.

QUICK TIP: Bookmarks make lovely, literate gifts. Collect colorful flowers, press them, and when they're dry, glue the petals on both sides of the marker and cover with clear adhesive-backed plastic. Oh, and don't forget about class pictures! Grandma and Grandpa would love to keep track of their grandchildren and the page number at the same time!

If Your Youngest Says, "But I Can't Read Yet!"

Say, "No problem. What's your book about?" She may look at the pictures and say, "*Puppies!*" Hand her some paper and crayons and cheerfully encourage her to draw some puppies. Any kind of puppies. And when you're reading to her later that night, stop at some point in the book and say, "Time to stop. Where's that marker so we can finish this tomorrow night?" She'll leap at a chance to use her creation. (You can always then take out her favorite poetry book and read one or two poems so that your time together is not cut short.)

🖐 On the back of the bookmark draw a series of horizontal lines. Encourage the kids to write down the titles of the books they've read as they go along.

These themed bookmarks are fun to handle and a dynamite way for your kids to keep track of their favorite books and subjects.

Firestarters and Paper Twists

Sometimes as I'm pulling candle stubs from candlesticks after the end of the holidays or a meaningful birthday, I think about how another lovely and exciting time has passed. I pick through the waxen leftovers and remember the special moment all over again.

Those candle bits can also continue to offer pleasure and maybe even create some additional lasting memories—as firestarters.

HERE'S WHAT YOU'LL NEED:

Nature finds such as bark, twigs, and pinecones

Candle and crayon stubs, extra paraffin if needed

Tin can

Saucepan

Muffin tray

Paper muffin liners

Wicks (from the craft store)

Newspaper

Children love watching one thing transform into another. It has a certain wizardry. So gather your children together and have them stand by, hands off, eyes wide. Oh, but first . . .

LET'S GET STARTED:

❧ Take a stroll outside to pick up some of nature's treasures such as pinecones, bark, twigs, and leaves. A bit of nature and a host of memories make a wondrous combination.

❧ An adult should put the candle and crayon stubs in a tin can and place it in a saucepan with a few inches of water. Turn the heat to medium. It won't take long for the wax to melt—keep an eye on it at all times. The wax is flammable. Carefully remove the old wicks as the candles melt.

❧ The kids may fill the muffin tray with paper liners.

❧ An adult, using a pot holder, should lift up the tin can and pour about half an inch of wax into each cup.

❧ Now consider your wicks. If you have a longer one from an old candle, you might want to use that, or you might prefer some fresh ones from the craft store. In any event, wind a wick around a pinecone and insert it into a cup, or simply place a wick with one end into the wax.

❧ Pick through your outdoor finds and design an arrangement, quickly placing a few twigs, leaves, and bark into the rapidly drying wax.

FOLD A NEWSPAPER
OVER AND OVER AND OVER
INTO A LONG STRIP

TWIST
IN THE
MIDDLE

KEEP
TWISTING...
THEN TIE

🖐 Once you're finished with your nature collage, add a little more liquid wax to the firestarters if you wish.

🖐 Rest a few of your firestarters in a straw basket . . . and then here comes an idea my father taught me.

🖐 Fold a newspaper in a long strip over and over and over and then twist it in the center, again and again, and then tie the two ends together, halfway down, with a string.

🖐 Place this paper firestarter in the basket along with your wax firestarters, and you will have a lovely, useful, and heartwarming gift!

To use, an adult places a firestarter underneath the kindling in the fireplace and lights it. The firestarter will ignite the kindling quickly.

QUICK TIP: Scented candles are especially nice. They will create a wonderful aroma as you both create the firestarters and use them.

A WARM
WELCOME
TO THE
NEIGHBORHOOD!

Create-A-Toy

"May we go to the store?"

How often have parents heard that question on rainy days, on an empty Saturday afternoon, or even on any school day after three? Wouldn't it be fun to say, "Let's not go to the store . . . let's make a toy ourselves!" Toys children make are not only fun, they also represent an accomplishment. A TIC-TAC-TOE BACKPACK somehow inspires more play than a manufactured set. Or sit down with your kids and create a few STRAY-GLOVE MUSICAL PUPPET PLAYERS. Hands and voices will thank you.

And you will have taught your kids that the road to something new and fun can start right at home!

Cereal Box Puzzle Play

There's never enough room on the refrigerator door for all of the kids' masterpieces. It's fun to keep rotating them, but you don't want to throw away the old ones. And you won't have to. They just need a new function. A promotion, you might say. From refrigerator decoration to puzzle pieces!

TRACE AROUND THE CEREAL BOX ON BACK OF ARTWORK.

HERE'S WHAT YOU'LL NEED:

Photocopied photograph and photocopied piece of art (about 11" by 17")

Nine small, empty cereal boxes

Pencil

Scissors

Bright-colored packing tape

Glue

I remember when I used to cut down the middle of these little boxes on a trip, pour in some milk, and start eating . . . hoping it wouldn't drip . . . drip . . . drip. Well, now all I'm concerned with is that everything fit . . . fit . . . fit!

LET'S GET STARTED:

🖐 Lay the photocopied (and possibly enlarged) piece of artwork out flat, art side down, on a surface. I think it's best to photocopy the art because kids may feel a little unhappy

about cutting up the original.

🖐 Line the boxes up on the back side of the artwork to see how many it will take to cover the paper.

🖐 Draw around the box as many times as it takes to mark the rectangle pieces that cover the art or photo. Then cut out the pieces.

COVER THE BOX SIDES WITH PACKING TAPE

🖐 Now it's time to cover up all the printing on the narrow sides of the cereal box. Pull out a strip of colorful packing tape, put it out on the counter, and then place the box, with the open end down, on the end of the tape. Press down on that first side, then roll the box onto its second, third, and fourth sides until all are neatly covered. Cut the tape. Press down any extended edges around the box to give your puzzle a smooth, clean, bright look.

GLUE ART
TO
THE
BOXES

✋ Squiggle some household glue on the front of the box and press a puzzle picture piece in place. Do the same with another picture or photograph on the back of the box so that you have two puzzles in one. (You might want to use a photo on one side and art on the other so that when you lay the pieces out you don't get confused about which piece goes with what side.)

✋ Finally, sit down with your kids, mix up the pieces, and start puzzling it all out. For a little extra competition, try setting a timer.

QUICK TIPS: Recycle pictures from old calendars. They make wonderful puzzle pieces too!

I like to keep these puzzle pieces in empty orange, lemon, and grapefruit net bags. If you weave a string through the tops, you can hang them on a hook for easy storage!

Enchanted Snow Globes

There's something magical about a snow globe. It's like peeking in on a whole new world. My family collects them on our summer vacations. Occasionally we give them a good shake, turn them upright . . . and then we smile with the memories. Snow globes made with personal objects have their own special whimsy. Creating one from your child's collection of tiny plastic toys is a fun way to give old treasures an enchanting new life.

HERE'S WHAT YOU'LL NEED:

Clear jars

Matching jar lids

Aquarium sealant

Small rubber or plastic toys or figures

White or silver glitter

Baby oil

Little jars, big jars. Fat jars. Skinny jars. First you want to have a vision for your scene. A tall jam jar might accommodate that plastic bear figure. A baby food jar would make a perfect home for a little gray rabbit. It's all up to your child's imagination . . .

LET'S GET STARTED:

ꗇ Find a clear jar that suits your child's fancy. Fill the jar with water and shake to test the lid for tightness.

ꗇ Pour the water out, remove the paper label, and wipe the jar inside and out. Let it dry completely.

ꗇ Pick out some rubber or plastic toys to inhabit this imaginary world.

ꗇ Put the toy on the inside of the lid and lower the jar down over it, just to make sure it fits.

ꗇ It's time to use some glue. *But not regular household glue.* You can purchase aquarium sealant at your local pet store; it's ideal for this project.

ꗇ An adult should squeeze a little glue onto the center of the inside of the jar lid and press the little charm or toy in the middle. Let it dry for 24 hours.

🖐 In the meantime, choose your glitter. White glitter, silver glitter, or sparkles of any kind.

🖐 Fill the jar almost to the top with baby oil. (You have to leave space for your figurine.)

🖐 When the glue on the lid is dry, sprinkle about a quarter- or half-teaspoon of glitter into the jar. Then squeeze the aquarium sealant around the inside of the rim. Let it go inside the grooves to make a good, tight seal. Carefully press the lid down onto the jar and turn it as tightly as you can. *But don't turn it upside down yet!* This glue has to dry too!

🖐 When dry, gather your kids around and have a shake fest. Then hold still and watch.

QUICK TIP: While you're in the aquarium store, you might want to pick up a small package of plastic greenery in case your kids have a forest or garden scene in mind.

Tic-Tac-Toe Backpack

Waiting. No fun! I get impatient. Kids do too. So here's a way to make waiting more fun. It's perfect for the bus stop, the doctor's office, or the checkout line at the supermarket (especially if you find yourself in the wrong line!).

HERE'S WHAT YOU'LL NEED:

Solid-colored backpack

Fabric paints in squeeze bottles, or permanent fabric markers

Velcro squares

Two sets of five matching charms, buttons, or any other doo-dahs

Creating this tic-tac-toe-to-go game is as easy as *X*s and *O*s!

LET'S GET STARTED:

❧ Empty the backpack so you can flatten it out. Then choose a fabric color or two and squeeze on a tic-tac-toe grid. (You might want to draw it lightly in pencil first for some guidelines.) Let dry.

❧ Scrounge around in the button jar or in a game box that's lost some of its playing pieces and find two sets of five matching items.

❧ Place a small piece of

adhesive-backed Velcro in each square of the grid and put another piece on the back of each little charm or doo-dah.

❧ Finally, throw the pieces in the small pocket at the side of the pack and say, "Come on! Let's wait—and have some fun!"

QUICK TIP: Sometimes waiting at the doctor's office can be a little stressful. So try playing Guess the Alphabet to pass the time. Write alphabet letters on your child's back using your finger. If he's a real young one, see if he can simply recognize the letters. If your child is a little older, spell out an entire message.

Juice Lid Match Game

Ready for a game of concentration? It's great for when it's raining outside or the big kids are off playing sports and your preschooler is left behind. It's as much fun to make as it is to play, and it will keep her entertained for quite a while. First she gets to go hunting, then she cuts, pastes, and paints, and then it's time to put her whole mind to the job! Whew! But you watch. You'll be no "match" for her in the end.

HERE'S WHAT YOU'LL NEED:

Poster paint (optional)

Eight to sixteen juice lids with smooth edges from frozen juice cans

Four to eight matched pairs of little items that fit under the lids (pennies, paper clips, stickers, pictures, etc.)

Household glue or double-sided tape

LET'S GET STARTED:

🖐 It's optional, but many kids like to paint one side of the lids first to give the game a fun bright look.

🖐 While the lids are drying, go on a scavenger hunt for pairs of little objects. Look in drawers, small containers, and bowls that hold loose change and small household items. Test to be sure the things you find will fit relatively flat under the lids.

🖐 Turn the lids over and glue or stick on one item per lid.

🖐 When all the lids "have something to hide," flip them over, painted side up, and arrange them in rows. You're ready to go!

🖐 The first player begins by flipping over two lids. If the objects aren't a match, he turns them back over and the next player goes. If they are a match, the second player goes again. The winner is the player with the most matches at the end of the game.

Oh, and as I mentioned earlier, don't be surprised if your little one wins! Nine times out of ten, they do. I think our grown-up minds are just a bit too cluttered to ace this game!

Pourin' Rain Stick

I love toys that imitate nature, like rain sticks! Rain sticks were originally made out of old dried cactus. But you can make your own rain stick at home with your kids, using a mailing tube. The sounds are wonderful. So let a little rain fall into your life. Your kids will be mesmerized . . . and dry!

HERE'S WHAT YOU'LL NEED:

Old mailing tube

Ruler

Bright-colored, adhesive-backed paper, or poster paint

Stickers

Fabric or felt, if needed

Poster board or tagboard

Glue

Scissors

Funnel

Uncooked lentils, rice, beans, unpopped popcorn, etc.

You'll want to begin this project by decorating your tube. A tropical look is always nice. Lots of green leaves. Or maybe just a big sun to fool an unsuspecting friend. She'll pick it up, turn it over, and "whooooosh"—a sunny rainstorm!

LET'S GET STARTED:

✋ Have your kids measure the tube, then cut the colored adhesive-backed paper to size. Or, paint it if you prefer.

✋ Decorate the outside of your stick either by cutting out your own stickers from different-colored adhesive-backed paper or using construction paper cut-outs and glue.

✋ If your tube has metal ends, cover the inside surface of the ends with glued-on pieces of fabric or felt.

✋ To create the inside, measure a long strip of the poster board or tagboard the length of the tube. Then measure the diameter of the tube, adding half an inch. This number should be the width of your strip. Cut out the strip, then make a second strip the same size. Glue the two pieces together, right down the long center, and let them dry. You now have a kind of spine.

✋ Cut little slits along the entire length on both sides, one inch apart, without cutting through the center. Then bend the tabs backward and forward in an alternating pattern. This can be done in a random fashion. Some tabs can be folded down real hard. Some bent just a little.

① GLUE THE STRIPS ALONG THE CENTER ONLY.

② CUT SLITS ALONG THE SPINE.

✋ Take this spine and twist and turn it inside your tube. Scrunch it in all the way.

✋ Now it's time to pick your kind of rain. Use a funnel to make the pouring a little easier, and add several beans, seeds, popcorn kernels, and rice. Listen as you pour a little in each time. The "rain makers" will create distinctly different sounds. (Popcorn tends to sound like a very heavy downpour.)

③ FOLD THE SLITS BACK AND FORTH, THEN STUFF INTO THE TUBE.

✋ Maybe your kids will want a little of each. Or maybe they'll say, "Stop! That's the sound we want!" Add the desired quantity.

✋ Squeeze a little glue inside your cap and then quickly put it back on your rain stick. Let it dry.

✋ Hold your stick in a vertical position and then slowly turn it upside down.

Listen to the soothing sounds.
Now you can bring a soft comforting rain inside anytime you need it. How lovely.

QUICK TIP: To decorate your rain stick, you might also use tropical pattern wrapping paper or aluminum foil with big construction-paper green leaves glued here and there.

If Your Child Says, "I Think It Sounds Soooo Nice"

Enjoy a conversation about sounds. This toy evokes so many descriptive adverbs and adjectives. "It's shimmering!" "It feels so gentle!" "Everything is lightly falling."
Your child's words will sound as lovely as the rain stick . . . if not more so.

Potato People Planters

Our family loves potatoes. Mashed. Fried. Baked. We eat them right up. But there's something else we do with them. We dress them up! And we give them haircuts too. Earrings. The works.

It's kind of a family joke. We put them in the window sill garden and give our friends and neighbors a real chuckle.

"My, what personality your garden has!" people say.

They're right. And it just keeps on growing.

HERE'S WHAT YOU'LL NEED:

Potatoes

Potting soil

Grass seeds, alfalfa sprouts, wheat berry seeds

Doo-dahs such as ribbons, buttons, junk jewelry

What's really funny is the way these potato people seem to come to life!

LET'S GET STARTED:

✋ Cut a little piece off the bottom of a potato so that it's flat and can stand.

✋ Cut a small piece off the top, about half an inch down.

✋ Then, with a potato or carrot peeler, scoop out a little cavity in the potato the perfect size for planting.

✋ Have your kids put some potting soil in the "planter" and press it in well.

✋ Choose some seeds. Anything that germinates quickly will do, such as grass seed, alfalfa sprouts, and wheat berry seeds. Sprinkle them on top. You don't have to cover with soil.

❧ Water the planting really well and continue misting the soil every day.

❧ In two or three days the seeds will begin to sprout.

❧ Now comes the funny part. Dress up the potato people any way you'd like. Take two buttons and push them into the sides of the potato for ears. Take two earring studs and use them for eyes! Try wrapping an old piece of necklace around your potato for a lovely belt. Do you have a dog? Use a pipe cleaner as a tail! Exercise your ingenuity!

❧ Set the potato people by a sunny window. Watch their "tresses" grow in!

❧ . . . and the even funnier part. Turn beautician. Give Dad's hair a trim. Give the baby a sweet look by gathering all her hair together and tying it on top with a bow! The teenager in the family? Well, what's his dream cut? Short on one side, long on the other? Totally scraggly? Buzz cut? Let him go to it.

QUICK TIP: For quick hair growth, put a little plastic wrap over the planted and watered potato top until the seeds sprout. You'll be styling away in no time. By the way, keep the potato people in a cool, dry place.

Scooper Fun

This is a wonderfully versatile toy. Especially when you're at the beach. Need a shovel? You've got one. Want to play a game of catch? You've got that too. All you need is clean laundry.

Huh?

HERE'S WHAT YOU'LL NEED

Two 2-quart (or larger) plastic laundry detergent bottles with side handles

Scissors

Stickers

Sock

Sand

Next time you're headed off to the beach and your kids say, "I can't find the other paddle for the beach ball!" just smile. Then reply, "Have we used up the laundry detergent?" While your children flash you a look of complete confusion, fish around under your sink or in the recycling bin for a plastic laundry detergent bottle. (You might want to think about pouring the contents of an almost empty container into a smaller plastic container so that you can get this activity on the road.)

LET'S GET STARTED

❦ Wash the two bottles and remove paper labels.

❦ With a pair of sharp scissors, an adult

You've got your shovel!

And your ball catcher. But uh-oh. In the middle of a great game of scooper catch, the whiffle ball disappears into an unexpected wave. Is the game over? *No!*

🐾 Remove the lid and cup a sock around the mouth of the container.

🐾 Pour some sand into the scoop so that it works as a funnel, filling the bottom of the sock.

🐾 When your "ball" is the size you would like for tossing, tie a knot in the sock. Replace the lid.

🐾 Stand up, put the sock in one scoop, give the other scoop to a friend, and toss the ball!

Oops! Well, it does take practice, you know.

QUICK TIP: If your kids are a little older and skilled ball players, you might want to consider making the opening of the scoop a bit smaller for more of a challenge.

CUT ON
DOTTED LINES

should cut off the base of the bottle. It's easier to do than it might look. Dig the tip of the scissors into a point along the line of the base and then just start cutting.

🐾 On the handle side of the container, draw a big "U" shape where the bottom of the "U" meets the handle.

🐾 Again, an adult should cut this shape out. Soften the edges by trimming off and rounding the sharp corners.

🐾 Decorate with stickers.

Curtain Costume Calls

Julie Andrews had a wonderful idea in *The Sound of Music*. She secretly made play clothes for all the children out of curtains. Yes, she sewed and sewed, and suddenly everyone was delightfully attired.

But you don't need to sew to give your kids hours of dress-up fun. All you need are curtains. And even old ones at that!

HERE'S WHAT YOU'LL NEED:

Elastic

Safety pin

Curtains with casings

Headbands

Ribbons

Silk flowers with wire stems

These costumes are just perfect for children with fairy-tale fantasies.

LET'S GET STARTED:

✋ Maneuver a long piece of elastic (with a little safety pin on one end) through the casing of a curtain. When the elastic is all the way through, remove the safety pin, tie the ends together, and you'll have a gown or cape. Slip it around the child's waist or shoulders and, if necessary, adjust the elastic. For a cape, you'll want to keep it quite loose.

✋ For a voluminous veil, slip one end of one of your daughter's headbands into the casing, pushing on the rest of the material, inch by inch, until the entire casing is squeezed onto the band. You might want to try putting a little glue on the ends to keep the casing in place.

✋ Tie some ribbons around the ends of the band to float with the breeze.

✋ For a lovely floral tiara, place a few silk flowers around the band and add a ribbon bow here and there.

Your kids will be thrilled with the flow, float, and fun of it all.

QUICK TIP: A bright red or blue curtain makes a dynamic superhero cape. Help your kids cut out a felt initial and glue it on the back of the "cloak" for instant idol identification!

Stray-Glove Musical Puppet Players

Y ou can create lots of different puppets with mismatched missing-glove sets. One red wool right-hand mitten, one blue-and-white striped left acrylic glove.

Now you and your kids will bring these mismatched gloves together for some fun and storytelling.

Puppet Players

HERE'S WHAT YOU'LL NEED:

Two mismatched gloves or mittens

Adhesive-backed Velcro

Small, lightweight plush toys

Old earmuffs, bells, sequins

Needle and thread (optional)

Puppets are whimsical "characters" with which your children can act out a scene from their imaginations or favorite stories.

LET'S GET STARTED:

🖐 Have your kids slip on just one glove.

🖐 Cut a piece of self-sticking Velcro and press it firmly on top of the glove.

🖐 Put a corresponding piece of Velcro under the plush toy and press the tag down firmly on top of the glove. (You might want to sew the Velcro down for extra security.) Do the same with the other hand with another toy and glove to create another character puppet!

🖐 You can also take the "muff" off the earmuffs, put Velcro on the bottom of the muff, and stick it on the corresponding piece of Velcro on top of a glove. Sew bells on the muffs for eyes, and a few sequins over the glove, and you'll have an extremely furry and glamorous character!

"It's showtime!"

Music Players

Are your kids beyond the pots-and-pans stage of their homemade orchestra?

HERE'S WHAT YOU'LL NEED:

Buttons

Marker

Old mismatched gloves

Needle and thread

LET'S GET STARTED:

❧ Dump out the button jar and look for the jazziest, biggest, most colorful buttons you have.

❧ Stick a capped marker in one finger of a glove for support. Place the button on the inside tip, and help novice sewers learn to direct the needle in and out of the button holes safely (without sticking themselves!).

❧ When all ten fingers are done, bring your young musicians to a counter and start "tappin'!"

QUICK TIP: If sewing is too difficult, try using metal bottle caps. Just glue them on the tips of the gloves, let dry, and move on over to that counter. So what if you have a tin ear? This is perfect!

Atlas in the Kitchen

This section is about cooking. And it might not be a bad idea to include the globe or an atlas when you start pulling together all the ingredients. Cooking with an international twist is such a perfect opportunity to teach kids about geography, topography, and history. It's also a chance to talk about the rich and varied traditions that exist all over the world.

A BRITISH RIBBON SANDWICH is an excuse to sit down and chat politely about queens, kings, and monarchies in general and talk about what it would be like to have lived in a castle centuries ago. Amazing! A bit of cuisine to get you going, and you may be off on rousing political science and history discussions!

As the garlic cloves and chickpeas in MIDDLE EASTERN HUMMUS blend together, questions may abound! "The Middle East is in the middle of what?"

You name the recipe. Then listen.

Where's Sweden? How do lingonberries grow?

So that's Africa! Peanuts grow there too?

Does any other country have "British tea"?

What is the Hopi Nation? Can I see it?

Put out a little plate of stuffed potatoes and suddenly everyone is munching on SPANISH TAPAS and learning something new about the world.

But there's something else too.

In many families the kitchen is the center of activity. While one person is cooking or talking on the phone, another is doing his homework or reading over the mail. A challenging game of checkers might even be going on at the kitchen table!

When you combine fascinating cuisine with an already active and involved family, you end up with a wonderfully fulfilling and filling experience!

Of course, things can get really quiet in the kitchen too. When yummy EAST INDIAN BARFI FUDGE finds its way into little fingers, there never seems to be a reason for talking!

Basic Kitchen Safety

Before we get to the recipes, I want to mention a few safety tips. They are especially important if you have little ones around. I know that when I start cooking it's sometimes easy for me to zone into what I'm doing. But when kids are involved, they must be the focus. These are the safety measures I always keep at the top of my mind:

❧ When your four-year-old wants to drag over a stool to get a sniff from a pot whose cover you are about to lift, explain that steam burns. "Not yet, honey," you might say "Stand here with me in the middle of the kitchen and take a deep breath instead. Now how does it smell?" Then describe it together.

❧ Remember that hot oil pops.

❧ If you are moving a saucepan of boiling water, make sure children are not in your path.

❧ Keep a number of pot holders within easy reach. Your older kids probably know to use them. But if the holders aren't readily in sight, impatience could get the better of them.

❧ If you want to teach your older children to cut something with a sharp knife, always supervise until they are confident and adept using the tool. An open dish towel set under a cutting board helps prevent the board from slipping while cutting.

Now have an enjoyable, safe time!

African Peanut Stew

After I graduated from college, I worked as a teacher in Congo, Africa. The village where I lived was right on the equator. There were so many delicious foods growing everywhere. Papaya, mango, and groundnuts were among my favorites! This groundnut stew is an adaptation of a tasty dish that was often prepared for celebrations. Families would sit around the cooking pot and tell stories of their past, and now, when we make it in our home, my family does the same.

HERE'S WHAT YOU'LL NEED:

One whole chicken, cut into pieces (remove the skin to cut down on fat)

½ c. flour

2 Tbsp. peanut oil

1 14-oz. can tomatoes, drained

1 tsp. salt

1 sweet potato, peeled and cubed

1 large onion, chopped

¼ c. chilies, mild or hot to taste (optional)

2 c. chicken stock, canned or fresh

½ c. chopped fresh peanuts

3 hard-boiled eggs

LET'S GET STARTED:

🖐 Preheat the oven to 350°F.

🖐 Dust the chicken with flour and fry the pieces in oil for a couple of minutes in a large frying pan, until golden brown. The chicken doesn't need to be cooked through.

🖐 Place the chicken in a casserole and add the tomatoes, salt, sweet potato, onion, and chilies. Pour the chicken stock over the chicken and sprinkle with the chopped peanuts.

🖐 Cover and place the casserole in the oven for one hour.

Serve with Verve:

When the dish is finished cooking, slice the hard-boiled eggs in half and arrange them around the edge of the casserole. The colors are unbeatable, and the flavor combo a real treat.

If Those Young Taste Buds Are Super-Duper Delicate

Some people like their chilies mild, others hot. Many kids prefer to skip them altogether! Luckily, you don't need chilies to enjoy the delicious flavors of this dish. If your kids would rather not have them, better to put the chilies on hold and make a dish the whole family can gather around.

Italian Pasta

Pasta is a favorite national dish of Italy, where it is typically cut into a variety of unique shapes. But not just in Italy. Kids everywhere love pasta! Mysteriously, though, some claim to love linguine but not spaghetti, or shells but not elbows. And no matter how many times adults have tried to explain that it's all the same thing, children have insisted, "*No! It tastes different!*" Well, here's your chance to check it out. You and the kids can cut this dough into a variety of different shapes right before your eyes!

Of course, there's no guarantee your kids will see it any other way. Maybe their taste buds do respond to form as well as content.

HERE'S WHAT YOU'LL NEED:

1 c. flour

1 egg

1 Tbsp. water

As experienced Italian cooks will tell you, the size of the egg and the moisture content of the flour will determine exactly how much flour is needed. The rule is: add as much flour as can be absorbed by the egg and water.

LET'S GET STARTED:

🖐 Mound the flour on a work surface and make a deep "volcano."

🖐 Break the egg into the volcano and add water. (Little ones love breaking the eggs.)

🖐 Beat the egg and water lightly with a fork, being careful not to break down the volcano walls.

🖐 Gradually begin to incorporate flour from the inner sides of the volcano. (This is a good job for kids to exercise their motor skills and patience.)

🖐 Continue to stir in the flour until the dough is stiff. Eventually, using your hands, knead the dough until it's smooth.

🖐 Refrigerate for about an hour for easier handling when rolling and cutting.

🖐 To shape the dough, use a pasta maker, or roll it out with a rolling pin until it's a thin sheet. Cut the dough into noodles with a pastry wheel or pizza cutter. Of course, you don't have to stick to standard forms. Using a small table knife, try different "kid" shapes like wiggly lines or little triangles or stars or mini-clouds!

🖐 An adult should boil the pasta in water for two to three minutes only. Homemade noodles are softer than the dried pasta that comes in packages.

Now if your kids say, "I like the squiggly shapes better!" as they humorously slurp the pasta into their mouths, you'll have your answer to the taste question. Maybe some forms are just a little more . . . fun. Period.

QUICK TIP: Excess uncooked pasta dough can be refrigerated in an airtight bag for up to four days, or frozen for a month. So the next time you decide to make some chicken soup, defrost the dough and try making little egg shapes! Or better yet, little chicken claw prints?!

Latin American Ropa Vieja

Little did I know as a kid when my mom whipped up a Sunday pot roast that she was really just an inch away from making this very popular Latin American dish. Ropa vieja is beef cooked until it is tender enough to shred. It practically falls apart by itself! Fittingly, the name translates as "old clothes" or "rags." This dish can be found as a staple in many countries in Central and South America.

HERE'S WHAT YOU'LL NEED:

2 lb. boneless beef chuck roast, trimmed of fat

1 onion, sliced

2 carrots, scrubbed and sliced

¼ c. fajita marinade

¼ c. chopped mild chilies

1 red pepper, chopped

8 flour tortillas

½ c. sour cream

2 Tbsp. chopped fresh cilantro

1 c. salsa

This dish roasts in the oven quite some time, but it's worth the wait!

LET'S GET STARTED:

🖐 Preheat the oven to 350˚F.

🖐 Place the beef, onion, and carrots in a six-quart casserole. Scrub the carrots well so there's no need to peel.

🖐 Cover the pan and roast for two and a half hours. That's right, two and a half hours—that's the secret. If you don't have a lid, cover the pan tightly with aluminum foil.

🖐 When the beef is very tender, remove from the pan and cool. Then, using two forks, shred the beef into "rags." The meat should just fall apart.

🐾 Heat up a skillet over medium heat. Pour in the fajita marinade. Spoon the meat into the pan, stir, and take a deep breath to smell that aroma!

🐾 Add a few chilies or red pepper if your family likes them.

🐾 Let's go to the flour tortillas! Heat up another skillet or griddle over low heat. Drop a tortilla onto the skillet until it's warm.

🐾 Remove the warm tortilla, fold it slightly in your hand, and place some of the meat mixture inside.

🐾 Now you're ready for individual tastes. Let the kids add their favorites. Sour cream, anyone? Cilantro? Extra onions? How about salsa?

🐾 Continue until everyone's got their own. And when they do, you can say to your family, "Enjoy! *Buen provecho!*"

QUICK TIP: Instead of dropping the tortillas into a pan, you can put your filled tortillas, wrapped in foil, into the oven to be lightly warmed.

Serve with Verve:

It's always fun to lay out the many garnishes in a collection of festive little bowls. People dip into this one and that. It's a little like inviting everyone to personalize their own cuisine! A thoughtful gesture.

East Indian Barfi Fudge

Kids may laugh out loud at the name of this wonderful cream-colored sweet fudge from India. It can be eaten as a snack any time of day. Indians frequently bring a prettily wrapped box of barfi fudge as a gift when visiting friends.

HERE'S WHAT YOU'LL NEED:

2 c. whole milk

2 Tbsp. butter

¾ c. sugar

2 c. blanched almonds, ground finely (using a small food processor or coffee bean grinder), plus several whole almonds

This is a recipe for the sweet tooth in all of us, regardless of our nationalities!

LET'S GET STARTED:

❧ Butter a large square of waxed paper.

❧ An adult should bring the milk to a boil in a large heavy saucepan over high heat. Stir constantly until the milk is reduced by half. It should take about 10 minutes.

❧ Add the sugar and butter.

❧ Gradually add the ground almonds, stirring continuously.

❧ Cook, stirring, until the mixture is stiff (about three minutes). It will have the consistency and texture of tapioca.

❧ Pour the fudge onto the buttered waxed paper. Spread it out evenly to a thickness of about half an inch. Let it cool and harden slightly.

❧ Cut the fudge into diamond shapes before serving. Press a whole almond into each piece.

❧ Nestle each piece of fudge on a paper lace doily and serve.

Serve with Verve:

Mangos make a delicious accompaniment to Barfi fudge. But they can be a little hard to cut. An adult should hold the mango upright and slice down along the long side of the flat smooth pit. Take this piece of the mango off and then score it across in a grid pattern, almost down to the skin but not quite. Then tell your kids to hold it between two hands, fruit side up, and press the skin up with their fingers. Little chunks will appear! Serve them in a bowl alongside the fudge for a most wonderful and unique taste sensation.

Swedish Pancakes

I've always enjoyed one of my grandmother's favorite dishes, Swedish pancakes. She didn't work from a formal recipe ("A little bit of this, a little bit of that," she'd usually say). I learned the basics, and now my family and I relish these pancakes for dinner frequently.

Unlike the thicker American flapjack, a Swedish pancake is more like a French crepe. In Sweden it is often served with a hearty bowl of pea soup for supper.

HERE'S WHAT YOU'LL NEED:

3 eggs

2 ½ c. milk

1 ¼ c. flour

1 Tbsp. sugar

½ tsp. salt

2 Tbsp. melted butter

¼ tsp. vanilla extract (optional)

Are you good at flipping pancakes? Here's a challenge!

LET'S GET STARTED:

🌿 Combine all the ingredients in a bowl with a whisk. Make sure there are no lumps remaining in the batter.

🌿 Heat a ten-inch nonstick skillet over medium heat until it is very hot.

🌿 Lightly butter the skillet and then pour in about a quarter of a cup of the batter.

🌿 Swirl the pan with the batter so that a thin layer covers the entire bottom of the pan.

🌿 Cook until the pancake is golden brown on the bottom (lift a corner up to check the color) and bubbles are visible on the top. This happens quickly. Flip the pancake with a spatula and continue to cook for about one more minute. These pancakes are big and quite thin. Don't expect perfection when you start flipping. They can be a little unwieldy at first.

🌿 Remove the pancake from the skillet and, if you'd like, brush it with a touch of melted butter.

🌿 Fold the delicate pancake into quarters.

If Your Kids Say, "May I Pour Maple Syrup on These?"

First give them a few choices. Fruit sauces made with strawberries, blueberries, or lingonberries (prepared in a sugar sauce much like cranberries) will give the pancake just the right tang, keeping to the tradition. But if maple syrup it is, then your kids have their own Swedish-American version.

British Ribbon Sandwiches

The tradition of "tea" started in England in the early nineteenth century when the time between lunch and dinner lengthened. People would get together around four o'clock in the afternoon to relax and talk around a bit of light nourishment. They'd sip tea and snack on delicate sandwiches and pastries.

How civilized.

Let's do it!

HERE'S WHAT YOU'LL NEED:

3 slices firm, thinly sliced white bread

2 slices firm, thinly sliced whole-wheat bread

3 Tbsp. strawberry-flavored (or your child's favorite) cream cheese

Think "proper."

LET'S GET STARTED:

❀ Spread the cream cheese on each slice of bread, making sure to get to all the corners. Stack them up neatly, alternating white and wheat slices. Press slightly as you go along with

the palm of your hand to make sure the layers stick together.

❀ Cut the crusts from the bread with a serrated bread knife.

❀ Slice the sandwich into one-inch-wide fingers (about three pieces). Be sure to hold the multi-layered sandwich firmly with the other hand while cutting so that the bread slices don't slip.

❀ Turn the slices on their sides so that the "ribbons" are facing up and place them on a platter.

Suggest that your children enjoy their ribbon sandwiches with a cup of tea. If they prefer, fill a teacup with milk instead. They'll enjoy the special occasion.

QUICK TIP: Create a mood. While they munch, read your little ones a tale of princes and princesses. Or suggest they slip on some of their dress-up jewelry. After all, this is a meal fit for royalty!

Serve with Verve:

Place a lace doily on the platter before displaying the ribbon sandwiches. Then, for a very gracious presentation, arrange the slices in a fan shape.

Jewish Hamantaschen

Hamantaschen is one of the traditional sweets of Purim, a festive Jewish holiday. Hamantaschen are tri-cornered pastries that hold sweet fillings such as honey–poppy seed, almond, prune, or apricot.

But don't wait for Purim. Enjoy these wonderful cookies with your family all year around!

HERE'S WHAT YOU'LL NEED:

¾ c. sugar

2 c. flour

2 tsp. baking powder

¼ tsp. salt

½ c. butter, cut into small pieces

1 egg, beaten

3 Tbsp. orange juice

Prepared fillings—poppy seed, apricot, almond, prune

Powdered sugar

It all begins with a delicious sugar cookie dough. Prepare this recipe, or use commercially prepared dough and skip to the rolling-out step.

LET'S GET STARTED:

🖐 Combine all of the dry ingredients and stir until blended.

🖐 Slowly cut in the butter until the mixture resembles a coarse meal.

🖐 Add the beaten egg and orange juice and mix until the dough holds together in a ball. Chill the dough. (This will make it easier to roll out.)

🖐 Preheat the oven to 400°F.

🖐 Lay a sheet of parchment paper over a dishcloth and sprinkle it with flour. (The dishcloth will keep the paper from sliding around.) Set the dough on the paper and sprinkle it with a little more flour. Cover the dough with another sheet of parchment.

🖐 With a pastry roller, roll out the dough to a thickness of about ⅛ inch.

🖐 With a three-inch round cookie cutter (preferably with a handle for little hands), a tin can, or a drinking glass, cut out round shapes. Separate the circles from the extra dough and place them on a separate sheet of parchment paper.

🖐 Scoop a teaspoonful of your favorite fillings onto the center of each circle.

🖐 Fold the edges of the circle inward toward the center to form a triangle. Lightly pinch together three edges of the three joined sections of dough until they're almost closed, leaving a small opening in the center for the filling to peek through.

🖐 Bake on a parchment-lined cookie sheet for about 20 minutes. Cool the hamantaschen on a rack.

🖐 Dust lightly with powdered sugar before serving to give the pastries a beautiful and festive look!

QUICK TIP: Save the tin can you used to cut a circle and bend it into various shapes to use with other cookie recipes. For example, if you squeeze two sides in gently, you'll have a football shape, ideal for Super Bowl cookies.

Serve with Verve:

The Israeli colors are sky-blue and white. Why not place your hamantaschen in a basket draped with one blue and one white napkin? It's a nice presentation!

Native American Fry Bread

'm always reminded of fairs and local festivals when I whip up this treat. My kids love it. It's a Native American tradition of the southwest.

Fry bread is a thin round of fried dough puffed like a giant doughnut without the hole in the middle. It can be a tasty complement to all kinds of main dishes, and drizzled with honey and powdered sugar, it turns into a scrumptious dessert.

So find the southwest corner of the United States on the map to get situated, look up in the dictionary or encyclopedia the history of adobe homes (for a little culture), and start cookin' (for a festive goody).

HERE'S WHAT YOU'LL NEED

2 c. flour

1 Tbsp. baking powder

1 tsp. salt

¾ c. warm water

1 Tbsp. oil (peanut oil is best)

Peanut or other vegetable oil for frying

Honey

Powdered sugar

Announce: "Anyone want a special treat?"

LET'S GET STARTED:

🖐 Mix the dry ingredients together in a large bowl.

🖐 Stir in the water and oil. Kids will want to dip their hands into this gooey mixture.

🖐 Knead the dough (it's going to be a little sticky at first) until it is smooth and elastic. Shape the dough into a ball, place it in a sealable plastic bag, and refrigerate it for about an hour.

🖐 Take it out of the refrigerator and shape small globs of the chilled dough into about 12 small balls and flatten them with your hands.

🖐 Roll the flattened balls out into four- to five-inch circles. Let the circles sit for five minutes and roll them again. They should spread to seven or eight inches, creating a fairly thin disk.

🖐 An adult should heat about one and a half inches of oil in a deep skillet to 375°F. Slide the dough circles, one at time, into the oil. Leave the dough in for one minute on each side. It should turn to a nice light brown color. Be sure your kids step away from the pan for this step. Hot oil can spatter.

✺ Remove the fry bread from the oil with tongs and drain it thoroughly on a paper towel.

✺ Drizzle honey on the fry bread and dust with powdered sugar.

Serve with Verve:

Serve each fry bread wrapped in a bright festive paper napkin and send your kids out into the sun to enjoy the day. Expect a few of the neighbors to "just drop by" when they get a whiff!

American Chocolate Roses

Chocolate modeling clay is made by combining melted chocolate and light corn syrup. American pastry chefs invented the recipe for this delicious edible clay to make garnishes and unique decorations for their spectacular creations. I've been using it to intrigue my guests *and* keep my kids busy when company is due.

HERE'S WHAT YOU'LL NEED:

10 oz. semisweet chocolate chips

⅓ c. light corn syrup

Waxed paper

Do keep in mind that almond bark or butterscotch chips or colored candy disks can be substituted for the chocolate. Whatever you choose, the recipe is the same.

LET'S GET STARTED:

🖐 Melt the chocolate in a microwave-safe dish in the microwave oven for about one minute.

🖐 Check to see if the chocolate is completely melted. If it isn't, put it back in for another 30 seconds, stir again, and if it's still not ready, another 30 seconds. If you don't have a microwave, use a double boiler. Put hot water in the bottom pan, place another pan on top with the chocolate, and keep stirring! Remove from the heat.

🖐 Add the corn syrup to the melted chocolate. Stir. The lovely smooth liquid chocolate will turn into a clay consistency.

Now it's time to make chocolate clay!

🖐 Put a piece of waxed paper on a cutting board or countertop and scoop the chocolate mixture onto it. Spread it around with your fingers, making it as even as you can until it's about half an inch thick.

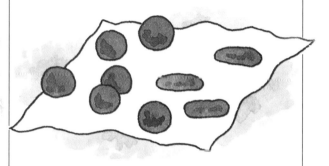

🖐 Cover the chocolate loosely with waxed paper and let it rest for at least a couple of hours or overnight. The clay will become very pliable. Perfect for molding.

🖐 Take off a little corner at a time. Roll it into a ball a bit bigger than a pea but a tad smaller than a marble. I'd say the size of a garbanzo bean is perfect.

🖐 Line up 10 of the little balls about an inch apart on the waxed paper and explain to your kids that these are going to be the petals of a rose. Then cover the little balls with a sheet of waxed paper.

🖐 Press down hard with your thumb to spread out the clay. Aim for the size of a half-dollar.

🖐 It's time to create the rose shape. Remove one disk and curl it into a tepee shape, narrow at the top and wider at the bottom.

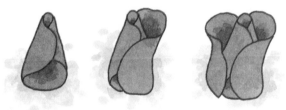

✋ Wrap the next disk around the opening of the tepee as if you were making it a little door. The third disk goes at the back of the tepee. The fourth along the side. Bend back the edges of the disks ever so slightly. Don't worry if little slits appear because they will make the petals look more natural. Add as many of these disks as you'd like.

✋ When you're done, let the roses harden before eating them up, or immediately put them on a cupcake or dreamy torte.

QUICK TIP: This is first and foremost chocolate *clay.* So go ahead and try other shapes as well. A tennis racket with crisscross lines carved with a toothpick. Little baskets that you can fill with tiny candies. Or how about . . . chocolate inchworms?!

Serve with Verve:

Line a small basket with some paper or plastic straw and fill with fresh chocolate and butterscotch roses. Wind a ribbon around the handle. It makes a gorgeous gift, blooming with creativity.

French Marzipan Potatoes

The French are famous for their *trompe-l'oeil* or "trick of the eye" cuisine. One food is made to look like another. A famous example is the candy truffle, made of chocolate, in the shape of a mushroom-like root.

This marzipan potato (not like any potato you've ever eaten, I can assure you!) is another *trompe-l'oeil*. The "skin" of this potato is marzipan almond paste, a candy made of ground almonds that is very popular in France. The body of the potato is a scrumptious chocolate cake mixture.

"Some potato," your child will say as he chomps happily away. "I love vegetables."

HERE'S WHAT YOU'LL NEED:

2 c. finely crumbled chocolate cake

½ c. chopped walnuts

¼ c. apricot preserves

1 7-oz. roll almond marzipan paste (in the baking section of the grocery store)

¼ c. cocoa powder

¼ c. slivered almonds

Tell everyone it's time for their vegetables.

LET'S GET STARTED:

🖐 In a large bowl combine the cake crumbs with the walnuts and apricot preserves. Mix it all up with your hands.

🖐 Shape approximately a quarter of a cup of

WRAP MARZIPAN PASTE
AROUND CAKE LOG

the crumb mixture into irregular, stubby, oval "logs." Wash your hands to remove all the crumbs when you're done with the shaping and get ready to "peel" those potato skins!

🖐 Cut the roll of almond paste into six equal medallion-type pieces.

🖐 Place one piece at a time between two sheets of waxed paper and roll out into a five-inch disk with a rolling pin.

🖐 Remove the waxed paper and wrap the disk around the oval-shaped cake mixture log. It should be nice and sticky.

🖐 Fold in all edges and press together to seal the cake mixture inside. Pull away any extra "skin" to use on another "potato."

ROLL IN COCOA POWDER
AND ADD SLIVERED ALMONDS!

❧ The finished shape should resemble that of a small russet potato, which has a naturally imperfect skin. Little bumps and dents make it look more realistic.

❧ Roll the marzipan-covered "potato" in the cocoa powder.

❧ Insert a few slivered almonds to resemble slightly sprouted potato eyes.

Serve with Verve:

Place several trick potatoes in a small basket or bowl and present them as a surprise dessert. After confusing everyone, slice them into 1/2-inch-thick sections and place on festive dishes accompanied by a triumphant "Ta-da!" Or should we say, "Fooled ya!"

Middle Eastern Hummus

From the Middle East comes a recipe for a snack or side dish known as hummus. There and here, it is often served with pita bread, the kind with a little pocket inside. You can fill it with cheese or meat at lunchtime or, as in this case, use it as a "dipper."

Kind of like chips!

Tahini (sesame seed paste) can be found in grocery stores near the peanut butter or in the international foods section.

HERE'S WHAT YOU'LL NEED

1 lemon

¼–½ c. olive oil

2 Tbsp. tahini

1–3 medium garlic cloves

2 c. canned chickpeas (garbanzo beans), drained and rinsed

1 tsp. salt

The kids will love this. Just toss things into the blender and let it whirl!

LET'S GET STARTED:

✌ Roll the lemon back and forth on the counter to get the juices flowing. Cut it in half and squeeze it on a manual juicer. Pour a quarter of a cup of the juice into a blender.

✌ Pour in the oil and add the tahini.

✌ It's garlic time! Pop out a nice big clove from the bulb. Press a spatula down hard on the clove, and give it a major *whack!* Peel off the garlic skin, roughly chop the garlic, and drop it into the blender. (You might want to add one or two more cloves, according to taste.)

✌ Toss in the chickpeas and salt and then give everything a spin!

✌ Chill until ready to serve.

✌ Heat the pita bread in a microwave oven for about thirty seconds or in a 350°F. oven for about five minutes until lightly toasted.

❦ Use a pizza cutter or knife to cut the bread into bite-sized wedges, which can then be dipped like chips into the hummus.

QUICK (LOW-CAL) TIP: Chicken stock can be used as a thinner instead of oil.

Serve with Verve:

Try surrounding a cup of hummus with sliced vegetables for dipping. It's a great way to introduce a few more nutritious foods into your child's diet. Or scoop out a beautiful green pepper and fill it with hummus. Oooooorrrrr . . . hummus makes a nice sandwich too. Spread it inside a pita bread, add some alfalfa sprouts, lettuce, and tomato, and you'll have a delightful meal.

Spanish Tapas

Do your kids snack all day? In our house we call it grazing. When they do, it's fine as long as their quick forays into the kitchen are healthy ones.

Spanish tapas are hearty snacking heaven. They're a specialty of southern Spain, enjoyed between meals. Typically tapas may include a simple bowl of mushrooms, artichoke hearts, and olives, or the healthy and popular stuffed potatoes.

Kids will love these as an after-school pick-me-up. They're fun to make, festive to look at, and delicious to eat.

HERE'S WHAT YOU'LL NEED:

Toppings such as hard-boiled egg yolks, bacon bits, tomatoes, dill, onions, etc.

6 red new potatoes

½ c. sour cream

LET'S GET STARTED:

🖐 Take a few small bowls down from the kitchen cabinet and get started sorting and chopping the toppings. The results are always colorful. Since it's a nice idea to have all the toppings set to go, arrange them in separate bowls.

🖐 Scrub and clean the potatoes with a little vegetable brush. It takes only a minute or two.

🖐 Cut each potato in half and then trim a little flat piece off the bottom so that the potato halves sit upright.

🖐 Place them on a microwave-safe plate and cover with some plastic wrap. Cook on high for about four minutes or until tender.

🖐 When the potatoes are done and cool, use a melon ball scoop, or a teaspoon, and dig out a little pocket. (You can save the scooped-out part for a scrumptious Spanish omclct the next morning—just add a little onion and salsa!)

🖐 Now it's fill-'er-up time. Put a dollop or two of sour cream in each potato's cavity, go to the little bowls of delectable toppings, and design your own tapas. Use whatever you like—tomatoes, cucumbers, red onions, bacon bits, egg yolks, dill.

Carbohydrates. The perfect thing for your hungry grazers!

Serve with Verve:

When company comes, take a good-sized, festive ceramic plate and arrange the tapas in little groups, right up against each other. Your tapas plate might say, "Something for everyone! Dig right in!"

Chinese Wonton

have to admit, Chinese food in my house usually comes from one of those little white containers with skinny metal handles.

But not always!

Wontons, a dish that originated in China, translates into "swallowing clouds." The dough is made from flour and water and shaped into thin two-inch squares. It can be folded in various ways before cooking and is often filled with ingredients such as meats, cream cheese (the American way), and vegetables. Wontons can be cooked by steaming, boiling, or frying in hot oil.

Of course, no matter how it's prepared, taste one and you'll be on . . . cloud nine. What else?

HERE'S WHAT YOU'LL NEED:

Cream cheese (plain or sometimes I add chives)

Wonton dough squares

Peanut oil

Wok

Packaged wonton dough squares, commonly found in Asian markets, can also be found in the produce or frozen food section of your grocery store.

LET'S GET STARTED:

✋ Place a teaspoonful of cream cheese in the middle of a piece of the flat dough.

✋ Dip your fingers into a small water bowl and gently moisten the edges of the square.

✋ Fold the dough over the filling to form a rectangle and lightly press the edges to seal. Before completely sealing, "burp" the dough by gently pushing out the excess air. Kids love this part.

✋ Grasp each side of the folded middle with the thumb and forefinger of each hand and pull the edges down and together.

✋ Press and secure one end on top of the other using a dab of water between the two edges to form a seal. It will create a "bonnet" shape. The perfect size for a child's hand!

FOLD DOUGH
OVER FILLING

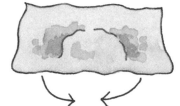
BRING TOGETHER

SEAL SEAM
WITH A DAB
OF WATER

❧ An adult should heat about one inch of oil in a wok, the traditional Chinese cooking pan, until it reaches about 350°F.

❧ Test the readiness of the oil by dipping in a chopstick. When tiny bubbles cluster around the chopstick and rise to the surface, the oil is hot enough for frying.

❧ A few at a time, place the wontons in the oil. After a short while you'll see them plump up and hear them begin to crackle as they turn a light golden brown.

❧ Using tongs or a long-handled woven-wire spatula, lift the "clouds" out of the oil and place them on a paper towel to drain and cool.

Serve with Verve:

As an appetizer, wontons are often dipped in a sweet and sour sauce. But for a yummy desert, fill the center with sweetened cream cheese and sprinkle with powdered sugar. Better than clouds, it looks (and tastes) heavenly!

Hikes and Bikes (and Car Trips Too)

There's so much to see and do in the outdoors. Even the tiniest details possess a bit of wonder.

Twigs, leaves, stones, streams, pebbles, and acorns.

I love to share the adventure of children wandering about in a wooded area enjoying the smells, sounds, and textures. It's wonderful experiencing how it all works together . . . how the trees look against the sky and the stream flows over the rocks. I rarely talk during such an expedition. I try to just let it, and everyone, be.

But I do try to keep that sense of nature's unity and camaraderie in these activities. NATURE BRACELET COUTURE can look as if the earth's many offerings simply flew onto your wrist. The FINE-FEATHERED FEEDER may make any child one of nature's architects. Using the treasures they find outside gives children a genuine appreciation of nature. They're on the lookout for the acorn nestled in the leaves, the pinecone resting by the tree, and that twisted twig almost lost in the shade of the fence post.

This is good, because when you're in the car taking one of those long family road trips, you're with your family in a very small space and nature becomes a blur! Unlike a nature walk, where spontaneity is everything, these trips take planning! A TRAVEL ATTACHÉ works wonders when the kids pack it with snacks, games, books, and a pile of pennies for trading, math games, or flipping pastimes. And a GEOGRAPHY JOURNAL gives kids a chance to reflect on the day and to keep it all fresh when the journey is over and everyone is back home.

Where you can design YOUR STREET BEAT PLAYMAT or get all wet doing the FAMILY BIKE WASH.

Out in the world. There's so much to discover, admire, learn, and do! All it takes is a pair of sturdy walking shoes or sneakers, an open mind, and family to share it with!

Travel Attaché

Lots of parents I know look forward to *and* at the same time feel hesitant about embarking on a family car trip. On the one hand, they have lovely memories of their own family adventures when they were kids, but on the other, they may have recently experienced some "backseat misadventures."

To hit the road on a positive note, find an out-of-use professional briefcase . . .

HERE'S WHAT YOU'LL NEED:

That old briefcase or attaché

A collection of your kids' "must-haves"

A little paint, a few stickers, decals

First of all, invite your kids to decorate their travel attaché. Let each of them leave his or her own personal stamp on it using paints and stickers. A painted initial, a few decals, a ribbon around the handle are a few possibilities.

LET'S GET STARTED

🐾 Your children's travel needs might be divided into categories. Let's try these three for now: Entertainment, Nourishment, and The Mind. Help them gather the necessities.

🐾 For Entertainment, you might include a cassette player and tapes, coloring books and crayons, even hand-held games.

🐾 For Nourishment, include healthy possibilities such as cans of fruit juice, yogurt, and cheese sticks.

🐾 For The Mind, select books, coins for on-the-spot game inventions (How Much Am I Holding?), brain games, and a list of license plate activities (The First Person to Find a Plate from a State That Gets Tornadoes Wins!).

There's no wrong way to do this when the kids get involved. Show them the briefcase, offer up some categories, and see what they devise for their own travel attaché.

Hush-Hush Safari

A walk in the woods is magical. It's a perfect time to just be. Be with yourself. Be with nature. And best of all, be with your kids and feel the togetherness.

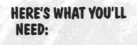

HERE'S WHAT YOU'LL NEED:

Just you and the kids and nature.

LET'S GET STARTED:

🖐 Feel the squishy mud beneath your feet.

🖐 Build a dam in the stream.

🖐 Construct a bridge with twigs.

🖐 Float leaves on the kid-made reservoir.

🖐 Collect pinecones, pebbles, leaves, and twigs.

🖐 Watch squirrels scamper up trees.

🖐 Lift up leaves and find little bugs.

🖐 Lift up stones and find bigger bugs.

No need to ask questions! Just see and touch and smell.

But most of all, notice where your child's attention is drawn. Help build the dam. Float a leaf. Look under that rock.

Give your child an interested and respectful and undemanding companion.

Remember, it's the little things that yield big results.

Fine-Feathered Feeders

It's so rewarding to look out a window and see a cluster of birds peck-peck-pecking away at the treats we've left behind. It's an especially lovely sight when the feeder itself blends in with the beauty of nature.

Your kids will love crafting this fanciful bird feeder because it offers so many possibilities. A pinecone here. Crisscrossed twigs there. Try a row of leaves on top and a few acorns on the side or at the bottom. Paint this side green. No, blue! Okay, both.

And when it's all done, every one looks different and wonderful!

Can you believe it? A bird feeder without a saw, hammer, or one piece of woodworking equipment.

HERE'S WHAT YOU'LL NEED:

Half-gallon cardboard juice or milk carton

Stapler

Pen and mug to trace

Scissors

Clothespins

Wooden skewer

Paint

Paintbrush

Household glue or hot glue gun

Twigs, leaves, acorns, dried flowers, pebbles, pinecones, etc.

Apples, oranges, bread

String (for hanging)

LET'S GET STARTED:

❧ First rinse the carton out. You don't want it to smell sour. Staple the carton shut along the top.

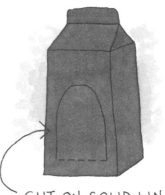

CUT ON SOLID LINE
FOLD ON DOTTED LINE

❧ Take a mug or glass and place it right in the middle of one side of the carton and, using a pen, trace a semicircle.

❧ An adult should cut out the circle, and then all the way down on both sides to within an inch and a half of the base of the carton.

❧ Tuck the flap into the bottom of the container and use clothespins to hold it down while you work. Cut out another opening in the back of the carton.

❧ Take a skewer (you can find these at grocery stores) and poke it through the top of the feeder. For the time being, rest the other end inside the little house.

← WOODEN SKEWER

HOLD FLAP INSIDE WITH CLOTHESPINS

🐾 It's time to decorate! Using a low-temperature glue gun or just regular household glue and a brush, start applying pretty leaves and twigs and sticks or pieces of bark wherever your imagination says they belong. Cover the entire feeder. You might add a few plastic trinkets or an old silk flower or two if the "space" seems right.

🐾 Grab an orange, apple, and hunk of bread. It's time for shish kebabs!

🐾 Cut the orange, apple, and bread into small chunks and thread them on the bottom end of the skewer that's been resting in the feeder. Then pull up on the skewer so that the end is once again inside.

🐾 Punch a hole in the top of the feeder, slip the string through, and hang from a tree. You're done!

Then watch as the birds begin to gather. Your whole family will nod with a sense of responsibility for their new feathered friends.

QUICK TIP: Little ones might enjoy making littler feeders from half-pint containers. And they can change the menu as well! Take a pinecone, roll it around in peanut butter until it's completely covered, then roll it once more in bird seed. Set it in the mini—bird feeder and hang outside. A feeder truly fit for the birds.

Your Street Beat Playmat

'll bet you your kids can easily map out the setting of their favorite television series. They know exactly where the main characters live . . . that they turn left to get to the water fountain and right to get to the stables.

But how well do they know their own neighborhood?

Here's a way to help children become familiar with where they really are in relationship to all the places that regularly touch their lives.

HERE'S WHAT YOU'LL NEED:

Old window shade

Markers

Ruler

Sponges

Acrylic paints

Basket of little plastic figures such as dinos, tigers, etc.

Bottle caps

Photos of familiar people

LET'S GET STARTED:

🖐 To make a great map, take a good walk together. Stroll down Main Street. Turn right down Buckout and head for the post office. Then left toward Gcordane's Market. Discuss the journey as you go. "Let's remember how close the gift shop is to the cleaners. Oh, look, the library is two whole blocks up from here." The point is not to memorize but to deepen a sense of relationship. The coffee shop is "across" the street. The stationery store is "three doors down" from the drugstore. It's a chance to teach that things aren't just "out there." They can be "located."

🖐 When you're back home, roll the window shade out on the floor and start with your home. You may want to center it on the shade to give the kids a clear idea of the surrounding areas.

🖐 With the ruler, start plotting out important places in relationship to your dwelling. Using your markers, draw in the streets and the town landmarks. The post office is two blocks down and one to the left, next to the cinema. Then there's the place where you get your double-scoop rocky road. Color or decorate the buildings any way you'd like. The ice cream parlor could have a big painted cone in the window. The post office might have a real stamp for a door.

🖐 Don't forget about any nearby lakes, ponds, or parks. Dip the sponges lightly into some acrylic paint and dab in bright colors for the water, flowers, and trees. Let dry.

🖐 Now spill out the basket of toys. It's time to bring the town to life. There's a tiger prowling the street right next to the supermarket! Wait until he finds himself eye to eye with the T-rex stomping down the steps of the library! And that bright green cowboy.

Look at him amblin' out of the corner store. Wonder which direction he'll run?

👋 To add a few familiar faces, take photos of friends and neighbors. See if any of the local shopkeepers will let you take a photo or two. Cut the people out, leaving an extra half-inch at the bottom to bend back and glue to the inside of a plastic bottle cap so they appear to be standing up. Now you've got human "players" in this neighborhood drama.

When you're all done playing, roll up the painted shade and save your portable town for another day!

QUICK TIP: Add a fantasy place as well. Would the kids be thrilled if there were a zoo in town? Draw one in! Don't forget a popcorn stand and a bench or two. Or maybe your kids would like a launch pad for the next shuttle. Pick a good spot, sketch it in, and watch for the next liftoff. If you don't have a tiny model of a spacecraft, you can cut out a picture from a magazine, mount it on cardboard so it stands up, and glue it to a bottle top before takeoff.

Batch-o'-Butter

Ask your kids where butter comes from, and they'll no doubt say, "The refrigerator!" Well, they may never really have thought about that before! It's always fun to answer an unasked question. It broadens horizons. "Let's make butter!" I announced one day. My kids looked at me curiously. How in the world was I going to do that? And with what? When?

We tried it together. It was a great indoor and outdoor activity!

HERE'S WHAT YOU'LL NEED:

Half-pint heavy whipping cream

Small clean plastic jars with tight lids

This is an activity you want to try when your kids are super-antsy. It'll shake out those wiggles in no time!

LET'S GET STARTED:

❦ Pull out clean plastic food jars and check to make sure the lids fit snugly.

❦ Pour the cream into the jar, leaving at least half the jar empty. Then screw the lid on very tight.

❦ Here's the outdoor part. Start shaking. Run around the yard and shake! Take a walk up and down the block shaking all the way. This requires real muscle! Shake for about 15 to 20 minutes.

❦ Pull out a bowl and place a strainer on top, unscrew the jars, and pour the contents into the strainer.

❦ Lumps of butter should appear. Globs of it! Delicious sweet butter. Buttermilk will drain into the bowl and you might want to save it for pancake batter, or just to drink. Spread a little butter on small squares of toast or crackers. It's such an old-fashioned delight!

You can add a bit of salt if you need a touch more flavor, or spread the butter on salted soda crackers. You and your kids will sit there munching away peacefully for a nice relaxing time.

QUICK TIP: Perhaps you'd like to serve your butter up with a little style? Press the butter into a plastic candy mold. Fill each little form (I have one with strawberry shapes) and put the mold in the refrigerator until the butter hardens. Then place a few butter pats on a fancy plate alongside a basket of mini-muffins and cups of juice. The young ones might want to invite their teddy bears to the party. You might bill it as "A Sunday Bear Brunch."

Nature Bracelet Couture

Walks through nature with children can be so satisfying. It's exhilarating to spot a bluebird or a perfect oak leaf or a tiny delicate pinecone. It soothes the heart.

But it can also decorate the admirer!

HERE'S WHAT YOU'LL NEED:

Masking tape or a strip of clear adhesive-backed paper

Nature finds

Before you go out on your walk, wrap a strip of clear adhesive-backed paper around your wrist.

LET'S GET STARTED:

🖐 Create a trail on your wrist. Pick up the tiny twig from the driveway and stick that right on. The beautiful maple leaf lying on the sidewalk ought to be a charm on your bracelet as well. Why not pick up a bit of sand from the lakefront and sprinkle it on a spot of wrist tape? And now, just look at that dandelion by the fence post. . . .

🖐 When you've filled your bracelet, wear it home and enjoy the fashion statement throughout dinner, if not longer. Reinforce the "finds" with household glue if you wish.

It's a splendid way to remind yourself that you too are part of nature.

After all, who's wearing whom?

Preparing for a Trip

Kids enjoy a trip so much more when they are part of the preparations. Having some sense of where they'll be and what they'll see helps them relax and feel more secure.

Gathering info "goes" a long way.

LET'S GET STARTED:

❦ Help your kids write away to the chamber of commerce in the towns or cities you'll be visiting. They can find out about key sights, festivals, industry, and other special points of interest.

❦ Visit the library and see if there are any books on your destination. A volume on the sights of Washington, D.C., will contain so many colorful images . . . and when your kids finally see the real thing, their eyes will absolutely pop! ("Wow! I didn't realize it would look *that* big!")

❦ If there's some dramatic history where you're going, filled with fascinating historical or folklore characters, take out some well-illustrated bios and explore the tales and myths of the locale. It will get your kids primed for a fascinating experience.

❦ Check out the Internet. Help your kids flip through a travel magazine, pull up some maps, or even explore different places to stay and eat. ("Look, Mom! This place has a pool, and nearby there's a taco restaurant!")

Kids love surprises! Once en route, throw in a twist or turn to your plans once in a while. They'll love it.

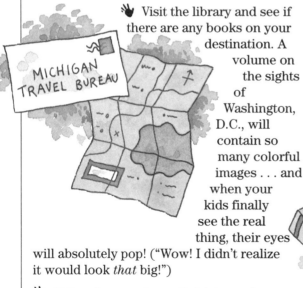

Geography Journal

If you're going on a family trip, why not keep "track"? A geography journal is fun to keep and even more fun to review when the vacation is over and everyone wants to relive the adventures.

HERE'S WHAT YOU'LL NEED:

Inexpensive spiral notebook

Colored adhesive-backed paper or construction paper (optional)

Maps, brochures, and assorted information about the trip

Glue, tape, and scissors

This is an activity you can begin before the trip gets under way. If your kids would like to jazz up the journal, decorate the cover of the notebook with some construction paper or colored adhesive-backed paper cut into shapes and designs. They might like to add a few drawings or affix beads and other doo-dahs too. When they're through, open the journal, with the kids all around, and say, "Okay . . . what's the plan?"

LET'S GET STARTED:

🖐 Suggest that each of the kids write in what he or she is most looking forward to doing. They might want to illustrate their thoughts with drawings of what they imagine something will be like.

🖐 Insert the map you'll be following and highlight the highways and byways! Or you might want to add a picture of your home as the official starting point.

🖐 During the trip it's always nice to date each entry so that when everyone looks back, they can trace the trip in their memories right along with the journal.

🖐 Ride tickets, matchbook covers, restaurant cards, and meal stubs are all little pieces of memorabilia you can glue into the journal . . . along with written impressions.

"The best fried chicken I've ever had!"

"The scariest ride I've ever been on!"

"The waterfall was so beautiful. Took lots of pictures. I'm going to leave room here to put one in when we get it back from the photo place."

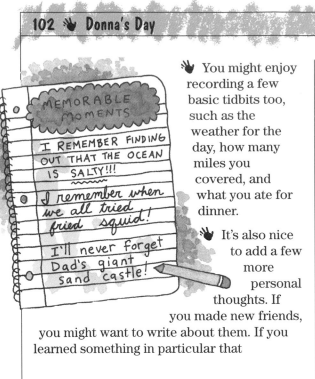

🖐 You might enjoy recording a few basic tidbits too, such as the weather for the day, how many miles you covered, and what you ate for dinner.

🖐 It's also nice to add a few more personal thoughts. If you made new friends, you might want to write about them. If you learned something in particular that fascinated you about another culture, you could note that as well.

🖐 Finally, don't be afraid to add some real 3-D inserts. A eucalyptus leaf, seeds from a pinecone that fell from an ancient redwood tree, an arrowhead—all can be neatly taped or glued into the journal.

When the journey is over, leave the journal out and open to a page that says something like, "Looking back . . . " Write about what you'd most like to do again or what meant the most to you about the trip.

After all, a good journal is not just about a trip. It's about a family who embarked on an adventure together. It's about doing and feeling.

It's about recording the wonderful moments of life.

Family Bike Wash

I love a good family bike wash. It marks a change in season.

It gets us all outdoors. It's something we do together with such happy anticipation of the ride ahead.

And everyone feels *so* useful.

HERE'S WHAT YOU'LL NEED:

Picnic lunches

Bicycles

Sponges and rags or paintbrushes

Pail of soapy water

Old towels

Safety helmets

Winter is just about over, and it's a beautiful crisp day. The kind of day that makes us know spring is just around the corner. It's time for a nice long ride.

LET'S GET STARTED:

🖐 Pack a picnic lunch filled with high-energy foods–peanut butter and jelly sandwiches, pasta salad, turkey heroes, fruit and nut snack mixture, and whatever else your family loves to devour!

🖐 Wheel your bikes out to the driveway or anyplace where soapy water can drain safely away.

🖐 Give out sponges or rags to the big ones and brushes to the real little ones. Spongers should gently wash off the grime, and the little ones can "paint it away" with water.

🖐 Carefully towel-dry the bikes to avoid rust.

🖐 Check to see if any tires need air.

🖐 Then pick up the helmets. Try them on the kids to make sure that the straps are adjusted properly and that they still fit as they should.

❧ A nifty way to prove how much your kids have grown is to have them sit on their bikes! Chances are, the seats will need an adjustment or two. Adjust the seat accordingly with a wrench, or with the levers if they have newer bikes.

When all is ready, grab that delicious lunch, throw it in a backpack, and pedal safely and cheerfully away.

Rollicking Rituals to Run the House

Rituals. Traditions. Aren't they kind of the same thing? Family life is built around doing a lot of the same things over and over, whether on a daily basis (Dad pours the juice every morning) or annually. (Bring out those BIRTHDAY PENNANTS!)

On the surface some traditions may seem a little routine. Even embarrassing. "Oh, there it is again!" your kids might exclaim each Thanksgiving as you unpack that dusty old turkey your child made years ago out of clay, buttons, and feathers.

But don't be fooled. Seconds later everyone will no doubt be smiling. Smiles that say, "I remember that! I can't believe you keep saving this! You must *really* love it. It makes me think of so many other Thanksgivings!"

Rituals, traditions, and even daily chores are reminders of where we belong. Where we are needed. What's expected of us as the years go by, and ultimately how glad we are to be a part of it all. The **PORTABLE HEIGHT CHART** doesn't simply mark a child's growth in height. Along with the charts of other siblings, it ultimately proclaims, "Well, will you look at how our family has grown together?" Sure, **SLICE-O'-PIZZA JOBS** remind your kids of the jobs that need to get done. But it's also a fun and loving way to help your children get those jobs finished! You may want to tote **CRAZY COUPON CARRIERS** when you are out and about on shopping trips. What better way to help kids learn how to count, comparison-shop, and save a little money too? A tradition, in other words, of family members standing behind each other.

When our children grow up, they are likely to take some of the traditions they've shared with us and change them a little. Add a few. Maybe leave a couple out. They will find their own strengths in the rituals that evolve in their own homes. And that's as it should be.

Every family deserves its own traditions.

Because every family and every person in it is unique.

Help Wanted: Preschoolers!

When the big kids are out earning cash—mowing lawns and baby-sitting—the little ones can feel left out. But they can be wage earners too! First, post the available positions. The application process is really quite simple.

HERE'S WHAT YOU'LL NEED

Poster board

Newspapers or magazines

Markers

Felt or craft foam sheets in different colors

Glue

Velcro

Be sure to hang this "employment section" in a busy part of the house so passersby won't forget to check! These are jobs outside of regular chores.

LET'S GET STARTED:

🖐 Cut out the letters E-M-P-L-O-Y-M-E-N-T or J-O-B-S and paste them at the top of the poster board.

🖐 Draw a line down the middle and with your marker write INDOOR and OUTDOOR on either side of the line.

🖐 Cut recognizable shapes out of the felt pieces to match jobs that need doing. Examples: a watering can for "Water the indoor plants," a garbage can for "Collect the

garbage around the house," a spade for "Dig up the dandelions," and a bottle or can shape for "Sort the recycling."

🖐 Draw in the details with markers.

🖐 Glue approximately four pieces of Velcro in a vertical line under each column on the board and the matching piece on your symbols.

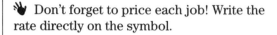

❧ Don't forget to price each job! Write the rate directly on the symbol.

Your little ones will feel all grown up, earning money just like the big kids. And it's a good way to teach them that while money doesn't grow on trees . . . there is money to be had from tending the garden!

If the "Employment Section" Starts to Lose Its Novelty

After a while your kids may look for new jobs. So make up some wacky ones!

Try posting the job of "lining up Daddy's shoes in his closet," or advertise the "fluffing every pillow in the house" position. Your kids might have fun and still do you quite a service.

Slice-o'-Pizza Jobs

S ometimes little ones get overwhelmed when confronted with a big job. Like picking up a messy room. It may seem easy enough to adults, but to them, well, where do they begin? It's easier when the tasks are broken up into chunks. That's what this activity is all about. Getting the job done . . . but in slices.

HERE'S WHAT YOU'LL NEED:

Dinner plate for a pattern

Tagboard

Scissors

Construction paper in various colors

Glue

Magnet strips (available at hardware stores)

Get your child thinking about pizza toppings as you cut out the basic food shapes together. Then discuss and decide the *three* key parts of the chore he needs to complete. Doing chores can be a game!

LET'S GET STARTED:

❧ Take a large plate, preferably 15 inches in diameter, turn it upside down on the tagboard, and trace. Cut the circle out.

❧ Divide the circle into three pieces (they don't have to be perfectly measured) and cut them out.

❧ Cut favorite toppings out of the construction paper: Red pepperoni circles, green pepper squiggles, or brown chunks of meatball.

🖐 Cut out the numbers 1, 2, and 3. While you are doing this, decide what part of the chore will be represented by slices number 1, 2, and 3. For example: (1) shoes in the closet, (2) clothes in the hamper, and (3) action figures in the basket.

🖐 Glue the numbers on each slice and then add whatever toppings your child would like on his pizza slices.

🖐 Put a magnet strip on the back of each slice, then put each one in a basket.

🖐 Watch your child speed into his room to get started! "Mom, my shoes are in the closet!" He'll run out to make sure slice number 1 is on the refrigerator door. Back he'll run to his room. "Mom, my clothes are in the hamper!"

Up goes slice number 2. "Mom! I put all my figures in the basket!" Before you know it, all three pieces of his chore will be done and an entire yummy pizza will be decorating your refrigerator door.

A job well done! Of course, by the time he's finished, he might decide he's hungry for a slice of pizza. I'd hand him the real thing, though.

As Your Child Grows:

Make an incentive with a few more pieces using a variety of themes. For example, use brown tagboard and make a chocolate cake. Or why not a banana? Surprise him with a special reward occasionally when there's a significant chore to be tackled. It'll keep him cookin'.

Reading Caterpillar

Reading is an important part of growing, but when spring and summer arrive, somehow books seem to end up on the back burner. There are so many other fun things to do during those longer days and warm evenings.

That's when an incentive program is just the thing! Here's an activity that will help motivate your child to pick up a book, finish it, and even give it some analytical thought.

A spirited, creative, bookish idea. What a wonderful combination!

HERE'S WHAT YOU'LL NEED:

Colored construction paper or paper plates

Scissors

Markers and stickers

Glue

Kids of every age (and that means adults too) can make this caterpillar grow. Turning pages—that's all it takes!

LET'S GET STARTED:

🖐 Cut colored construction paper in circles, about three inches in diameter.

🖐 Cut one circle four inches in diameter and draw a caterpillar's face on it. Be creative! Give it eyes, a nose, a mouth. You might want to draw an open mouth. This caterpillar needs to be hungry!

🖐 Attach your growing caterpillar to a wall, leaving lots of room for a trail of circles, and watch it grow.

🖐 Each time you read a book to your child, or your child reads one on his own, write the book's title on a circle.

🖐 Then decorate the circle with an illustration from the book. Was it about dinosaurs? Take a marker and draw a dino. Or use a dinosaur sticker if you have one and draw in a plant. Was it about a little boy who couldn't fall asleep? Draw a teddy or a pillow.

Also stars in the night. No need to be strictly literal. The pictures can be symbolic too!

❧ Glue the first circle onto the caterpillar head, allowing a half-inch overlap. Add the second circle, for the second book, to the first circle in the same way.

❧ For older kids who are reading lengthier books, encourage them to do a circle for every fifty pages or so they read.

❧ Don't forget to add a circle for your own books!

You're feeding the caterpillar books! How healthy!

If You Have an Avid Reader in the Family:

Suggest that for every two or three circles he adds to the caterpillar, he read a book to his younger sister and help her create a new circle of her own.

This will be a reminder to him that growing the caterpillar is a joint family effort.

Portable Height Chart

Ever mark your children's height on the bedroom door with a pencil and a tiny scribbled date? But then you moved? Or had a paint job?

I finally realized that a portable height chart is the only way to go. And grow!

HERE'S WHAT YOU'LL NEED

Piece of foam core or tagboard

Measuring tape

Paint

Markers

Get this going asap. You don't want to miss an inch!

LET'S GET STARTED

🖐 Mark "2 ft.," "3 ft.," "4 ft.," and "5 ft." along one side of a long piece of foam board or tagboard. (You might want to measure this together with your kids and mark it in pencil first, then copy over the markings with a bright felt-tip pen.)

🖐 Fill in the inches in the same manner and then hang the height ruler on the wall.

🖐 Encourage your kids to think of some milestone they might want to draw on the ruler that symbolizes a goal or accomplishment. For example, at "3 ft., 8 in.," she finally rode a two-wheeler! Draw in her red bike minus the training wheels. Or at "4 ft." he could finally ride the roller coaster! Draw in "The Wild Tornado."

QUICK TIP: Glue a measuring tape to the side of the chart instead of drawing in the marks yourself. It's quick and easy, and you and your kids can concentrate on jazzing up the drawings!

If Your Kids Are Real Little and Not Quite Ready to Illustrate

Paint handprints next to their heights. This way they can watch hands and height grow at the same time! (If you use foam board, you might want to stamp those palms on paper, cut them out, and affix them to the board with tape.)

Great Gold Record Award

Incentives work wonders. Provide a little perk, and a person feels appreciated and motivated to do more!

My kids can get so busy playing basketball that everything else in their lives can easily fall by the wayside. But somehow, with a very special perk, balance is restored in their multi-faceted, and sometimes quite musical, world.

I do it with a sign of admiration and appreciation.

And I do it in gold.

HERE'S WHAT YOU'LL NEED:

Old 45rpm records

Gold spray paint

Permanent markers

Velveteen

Old frame

Construction paper

Glue

Wide ribbon

Photo of your child

You will want to begin by setting a goal with your child. Is it 10 hours of piano practice? Is it learning a new flute piece within the next month? Agree on the target, and you're on your way!

LET'S GET STARTED:

🖐 Set up a system to keep current on his progress. Perhaps he'll log in the time spent practicing on a special daily calendar. Or maybe he'll create his own calendar and set up goals concerning the new piece for each week.

🖐 Once he's well under way, you can set to work preparing his award. Spray one side of the record with gold paint. Allow it to dry.

🖐 Write on the top of the record with a permanent marker the name of the instrument your child plays or the piece he's learned.

✋ Tuck a pretty piece of velveteen into a frame as background. Glue the record on the display firmly.

✋ Now it's time for the ribbon. Cut two circles, one bigger than the other, out of different-colored construction paper. Glue the small circle over the large one. Cut a fringe along the edges of the larger circle. Then attach a ribbon to the back so that it falls a good four inches from the circles. Write on the top circle the number of hours practiced or the child's name. Glue to the velveteen.

✋ Finally, attach a small picture of your child to give the award a very personal touch.

When your child has reached his goal, you might want to present it to him with grand ceremony. Gather the family around and say, "We're standing here together to honor someone who has achieved . . . " There might be a giggle or two, but then that's what you want.

A good time inspired by a job well done.

Invisible Librarian

Isn't it amazing how library books can disappear? They belong to everyone, and yet they can sometimes end up under a sofa cushion for weeks!

Well, here's a way to help keep track of loaned books. And it works!

HERE'S WHAT YOU'LL NEED:

Strip of poster board and marker

Glue or tape

Large basket

Looseleaf plastic pencil case with holes

String

Choose a place by the front door that no one can miss.

LET'S GET STARTED:

❦ Write the words LIBRARY BOOKS on the strip of poster board and attach it to the basket, using either glue or tape.

❦ Using string, poke through the holes of the looseleaf pencil case and tie it from the basket handles so that it lies on its side on the front of the basket. The perfect library card holder!

Tell everyone this is the place. The invisible librarian. When the book is finished, it belongs in the basket.

There are other people out in the big wide world waiting to partake!

Sick-Day Treat Tray

My kids love to be pampered when they're under the weather. I think extra attention helps with the healing, so I don't mind at all.

Especially when it comes to meals in bed. Such luxury!

Presentation is key. And there are so many tasty little possibilities. Below are my edible suggestions, but feel free to select your own.

HERE'S WHAT YOU'LL NEED:

Muffin tin with six or eight sections

Celery, peanut butter, raisins, dry cereal, cooked pasta, dried fruit, orange juice, frozen fruit on a stick

Toothpick

Construction paper

Think finger food. Think bright. Think smooth (for sore throats) and tasty.

LET'S GET STARTED:

👋 Take out the muffin tin, your handy tray.

👋 Spread some peanut butter down the center of a piece of celery and then line some raisins up, too, for "Ants on a Log."

👋 Put a spoonful of cold pasta in one cup, dried fruits such as apricots and apples in another, and a pile of dry cereal in still another.

👋 Sore throats will love small hunks of frozen fruit on a popsicle stick. It feels so nice as the sweet icy juice goes down.

👋 A little glass of orange or apple juice fits nicely in the final cup.

👋 Cut a small bannerlike shape from a piece of construction paper, write down the words "Get Well Soon!" and weave the mini-sign, along the straight edge, on a toothpick. Stick it upright and proud in the pile of pasta or dried fruit.

GET WELL SIMONE!

Then knock on the door and sing out, "Room service!"

QUICK TIP: Spread a little butter on a piece of toast, fill a squeeze bottle with some red jam or jelly, and "paint" a great big (sweet) heart in the center of the bread. It makes for a toasty, crunchy, loving treat.

If Your Child Wants to Go out and Play with the Other Kids

Nothing is worse than looking out a window and watching your friends have a grand old time outdoors. If your child is not quite ready to play a game of hoops, make him one he can comfortably play sitting in bed! Take a wad of newspaper and bunch it up into a ball. Tie one end of an eight-foot string around it. Set up a wastepaper basket at the proper distance and tell him to hang on to the other end of the string with one hand and take a shot with the other. After pulling it back by the string and shooting over and over again, he'll soon see it's not a bad way to hang on to "hoop dreams"!

Table Setting Placemat

When children are young, learning how to do a chore represents a "grown-up" accomplishment. "Look what I did, Mom! I put the cereal box back in the cupboard by myself!"

Setting the table is one fun challenge that requires lots of practice. It can get tricky! At first the fork may rest diagonally across the plate. The spoon may lie upside down on the left, and the napkin, unfolded, may rest half under (or half over) the plate.

So I came up with this table setting placemat, which will help kids along in the finer points of table setting.

HERE'S WHAT YOU'LL NEED:

A few different-colored sheets of tagboard or foam sheets

Glue

Velcro

Markers

When you call out, "Who wants to set the table!?" the kids will be eager to try out their new table setting placemat.

LET'S GET STARTED:

👋 Cut out an oval or rectangle shape. Or you can use a regular plastic placemat.

👋 Cut out a 10-inch circle from another sheet to serve as the plate. Your kids might think it's fun to use their markers to design a border.

👋 Draw a spoon, knife, fork, and napkin. Cut those shapes out.

👋 Put Velcro on the placemat at the appropriate places and on the backs of all your cutouts. (You might want to add a piece to the top of the napkin for the fork.)

👋 If you like, snip a few fun shapes or squiggles from another sheet and glue them on the mat for a little decoration.

QUICK TIP: Practice table-setting as part of pretend teatime. Your kids can first put the Velcro-backed cutouts on the placemat and then set the real things on top.

It's a fun and wonderful way to help your kids remember what goes where and adds to their sense of "I can do!"

Birthday Pennant

In our house kids' birthdays are so special, we serve them breakfast in bed! They can pick anything they want; fresh-squeezed orange juice, chocolate-covered doughnuts. But for something truly unique that speaks from the heart, here's an idea I got when I was living in Sweden. The day my daughter was born, the school where I was teaching flew the Swedish flag, and when I asked why, they said, "We're celebrating a new life!" So now, on my kids' birthdays, we fly a flag we've made together. A personalized birthday pennant that means, "We celebrate you!"

HERE'S WHAT YOU'LL NEED

Sports pennant (for a pattern)

Craft foam sheets or felt sheets in different colors

Paper

Marker

Glue

Paintbrush

Buttons, foil, shells, yarn, and other colorful little objects

Dowel

Ribbons and bells

Do keep in mind that your pennant doesn't have to be displayed only on birthdays. It can also be an "Anna made a big basket at the game!" flag, or a "Liam aced his final exam!" flag. It is a flag of celebration. The brighter the better!

LET'S GET STARTED:

❦ Lay the sports pennant down on a foam sheet and, with your marker, trace the outline onto the foam sheet. Then cut it out. This is an easy and fun task for the young one in your family.

❦ Outline on a piece of paper the letters of your child's name and trace around them on foam sheets, using different colors if you wish.

❦ Pour a little household glue into a shallow plate (it's easier for little ones to use this way) and, with a brush, coat one side of the letters. Glue them onto the flag.

❦ Now ask the celebrated child, "What's really special to you? Let's picture it on your pennant." Horses or in-line roller skating, chess or basketball.

❦ If the idea is quite difficult to create, figure out the best symbol for whatever your child holds dear. For example, a saddle for a horse, or a king piece for a chess set. (It doesn't have to be perfect.)

🖐 Draw the outline for the basic shape on another piece of foam and cut it out. Then *think fun details*. If it's in-line skates, use buttons for the four wheels. If it's a king piece, try shaping a crown out of tin foil. Draw lines on the basketball, or glue yarn on the saddle for reins.

🖐 Once everything is drawn in and glued on and allowed to dry for a few moments, cut some slits along the straight vertical side of the flag. About a half-inch in from the end, bend the flag and make little cuts about an inch and a half apart.

🖐 Weave the dowel through these slits until the pennant is flying straight up and down and out!

🖐 Finally, go into your ribbon basket, grab a few medium-length pieces (tie on a few bells if you have any), and secure them in a small knot at the top of the dowel so that the ribbons cascade downward.

And there you have it! A birthday pennant! Wave it around. Slip the handle portion of the dowel between books on a high bookshelf and let it dangle up and out. Or prop it between

the mounds of fruit in a large bowl. Stick it in a planter next to the dieffenbachia. After all, it's Flag Day in your house!

Quick Tip: Sometimes those symbols can be a little intimidating. Making it easy doesn't take away from the creativity. In fact, sometimes it heightens it! Use an old little kid's sock for the shape of a skate boot. Or simply create a little square checkerboard for chess. If making a horse and saddle are too much, just do four hoof shapes or a cowboy hat or a riding helmet. The pennant might turn into a guessing game. "Let's see, Laurie loves chocolate ice cream and tennis and . . . I get it . . . riding!"

Laundry Line Memories

When my kids go back to school in the fall, I like to sneak into their rooms and clean up. Toss out all that stuff they keep hanging on to but never touch. Old newspapers and magazines. Broken toys, even egg cartons. But always, as I'm doing this, I come upon a wonderful collection of mementos, usually in disarray! Under the bed. Stuffed behind a book or two on a shelf. Rammed behind the door.

So I pull them out and let the kids give them what they deserve.

Display space!

from that funny motel near the beach, or the bandanna from camp.

Oh, and do leave some empty pins on the rope. Your kids will come home from school and undoubtedly choose to add a few more items.

"Blanks" are your invitation to make it a "work in progress."

HERE'S WHAT YOU'LL NEED:

Rope

Clothespins

Mementos like ticket stubs, postcards, baseball caps

LET'S GET STARTED:

❧ String a clothesline across a corner of your child's room.

❧ Pick out the mementos and hang them up using clothespins. A banner, an invitation, a small map. Don't forget the soap wrapper

Crazy Coupon Carriers

When little kids think of saving money, they think piggy banks. That's certainly a start, but saving is more than taking what you have and putting it in a cute, fat, pink thing! It's also about watching how you spend money.

Coupons are a fun way to show children that if you're careful about how you purchase things, you can actually save a lot!

LET'S GET STARTED:

🖐 Open the Sunday paper and pull out the coupons. This is an activity that works for nonreaders as well as readers! Product recognition is at work.

🖐 Use the scissors to snip out any products you've seen around the house, or try some new ones.

HERE'S WHAT YOU'LL NEED:

Sunday newspaper

Scissors

Envelopes

Markers

Tagboard

Ask your kids if they'd like to go shopping. When you've got a few takers, invite them to sit down and begin. At home!

♨ When you're all done, take the envelopes and think of some handy categories, such as HOUSEHOLD SUPPLIES, TREATS, BREAKFASTS, SCHOOL LUNCHES, or DINNERS. Write these words on the flap side of different envelopes, but also be sure to cut out a little picture of a product that best represents the category and glue it on the envelope as well. That way nonreaders can participate in the next step. Mount these envelopes on a big piece of tagboard.

♨ Now start sorting. (This is a terrific way to teach a valuable skill.) Cookies and cake mixes go in the envelope marked TREATS. Cereals, waffles, and cinnamon toast get tucked into BREAKFASTS, and so on.

When you're ready to go shopping, check the list of what you need against the coupons you've collected and put the appropriate ones in a little pencil case. Tell your kids, "Come on! Let's go to the store and save some money!"

QUICK TIP: It might be fun with older kids to sit down and add up exactly what you've saved after each trip. Encourage them to keep a running chart. At the end of the month they'll be amazed at how quickly you've amassed just the right amount of money for a family outing!

Family Chore Chart

Most chore charts, the ones where the days of the week run across the top and the chores are listed down one side, don't take into account that family days are not predictable! What if no one's home for dinner because of a basketball game? Does one child get to skip her turn doing the dishes? Or does she have to do it the next night, thereby throwing off the whole chart? See what I mean?

So here's a new plan. It works great. Unless you have a gremlin in the house. (I'll explain later.)

HERE'S WHAT YOU'LL NEED:

White foam board cut in an 18-by-9-inch rectangle

Markers

Ruler

Six adhesive-backed plastic hooks in bright colors

Six metal rings (available at stationery stores)

Several plain index cards, cut into 1-by-5-inch strips with a hole punched at the top of each strip (one strip for each child for each chore and privilege—for example, for two kids and five chores, cut ten strips).

Before you begin, discuss with your kids the basic chores that need to be done around the house. Five or six jobs is a good number for starters. Also, you might want to add a category for the most-sought-after privilege.

LET'S GET STARTED:

🤚 With a black marker, print the chores across the top of the board. Draw vertical lines down the board to separate the categories. Under each chore attach a hook.

🤚 Print names on each strip, color-coded for each child. Let the kids choose their own color and, if they'd like, print their own names.

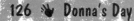

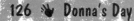 Have the kids loop their own names on each ring and then hang each ring on each hook.

 Then explain that the person whose name appears on top of the ring is "up" for the task/privilege in the category. When she completes the job, she is to flip her name over the ring so that the next child's name appears. Now it's his turn!

As for the gremlins? Well, kids have been known to take their names off one loop (washing dishes) and add their name twice to another (gets to choose any dessert). So suddenly someone's saying, "Hey! When's the last time Tim had sink duty?"

Nothing's perfect. Mostly, though, this chart works like a charm. Because not only is the method clear and fair, but the kids are involved in the process.

Family Connections

Family members. Sometimes we may take each other for granted. Siblings may pass each other in the hall with barely a nod. Or a son may leave such a short, matter-of-fact message on the answering machine that you're not even sure it was him who was speaking! Or grandchildren caught up with school and extracurricular activities forget to call Grandpa and Grandma.

And in a way all of this happens because of our basic trust and love for each other.

But every now and then I think we need to be intentional about reaching out and expressing how we feel. Siblings need to let each other know that, even though they squabble, they'd go to the ends of the earth for each other. REVOLVING ARTWORK FRAMES and WEARABLE ART give kids opportunities to do something generous for their younger siblings. And grandparents and grandchildren need to take the time to learn as much as they can about each other, because unfortunately they don't always have lots of time together. With the "G" IS FOR "GRANDPARENTS" alphabet postcard game, kids will be thrilled to exchange messages with distant family members.

"Family togetherness" is something of a catchphrase for time spent doing things as a unit, whether it's the immediate or extended family. But in this section these activities are meant to help everyone in a family feel appreciated, admired, and understood. Some are enjoyed together. Some are created for another family member. But all of the activities say the same thing:

"I value you . . . you are important to me . . . and there is no one in the world like you!"

"What's Baby Doing?" Sign

The arrival of a new baby in the house is so exciting.

As parents we're filled with the joy of it all. Exhausted too!

But siblings? Well, I remember when my brother first arrived I thought, "Hmmm. A great toy!" A week later I thought the toy was, well, so-so. By the third week I realized he was pretty noisy, not much of a toy, and he wasn't leaving.

Well, these feelings are very common. But to help smooth the way, try increasing your older child's sense of involvement with the new baby. The baby can be the object of your older child's warmth and interest as well. The more he's involved in monitoring what's happening with that baby, the better he may feel!

HERE'S WHAT YOU'LL NEED:

Poster board or oak tag or felt or fun foam

Scissors

Markers

Glue

Beads or sequins

Velcro strips

Felt and/or poster board

The idea is to create the kind of door hanger sign you see at hotels. You know. "Do not disturb!" Except, of course, the one you and your child create will be perfect for announcing what's really going on in the nursery.

LET'S GET STARTED:

🐾 You will want to start by making the basic shape of the door hanger. Hold a piece of paper up to the door to get the general size and shape correct.

🐾 Cut it out and then lay it down on whatever material you have chosen to make your sign. Using a ruler for the sides and a small plate for the rounded top (if you prefer that shape), neatly draw the outline with a marker. Then cut it out. Whether you've chosen felt or fun foam

THE BABY IS . . .

(which I prefer) or poster board, I would double the material before cutting out the shape and then glue the two sides together. This way your hanger will stand up better to eager little hands.

🖐 At the top of the hanger, cut a hole that is a little larger than the doorknob. If you're using a bendable material such as felt or fun foam, lightly fold the hanger in half lengthwise and start cutting out the circle. If you are using poster board or oak tag, you may need to cut cleanly through to the top of the circle, and then around it, so as not to create a fold in your sign.

🖐 Now decorate the edges of the sign with markers.

🖐 Place about three pieces of Velcro on each side some distance apart so as to allow for the display of three symbols at a time.

🖐 Discuss with your child the different things the baby does. You might come up with this list: she plays, eats, cries, sleeps, smiles, gurgles, spits up. Then ask your child what pictures he can think of to stand for each of those activities. Perhaps you'll decide on: a rubber ball for playing, a bottle for eating, a big tear shape for crying, a face with eyes closed for sleeping, a mouth smiling for that toothless grin, a tiny bib for spit-up. These are only suggestions. Your child might prefer a baby spoon for eating, or a teddy bear for playing or sleeping!

🖐 On your chosen material, draw the objects you and your child think will work best. Keep it simple! You don't have to be a terrific artist to cut out a bottle or teddy bear shape and add a few details like wavy lines for the milk or black circles for eyes. A crying or smiling face can just be a circle with two dots for eyes and a simple line frown or line smile.

🖐 Cut the objects out and glue a piece of the matching Velcro strip onto the back of each.

🖐 Finally, hang the sign on the baby's door and either leave a small basket filled with the symbols resting by the nursery door or place a few in front of the hanger and a few in back. Invite the older sibling to take a look at what's happening in the nursery and adjust the symbols with the correct ones facing out.

He'll start to feel so . . . attached!

QUICK TIP: When drawing details, just think *shape and color.* Cut a mouth out of red felt, a bottle out of white felt, a teddy out of brown felt, and a bib out of any color (try gluing on old shoestring pieces for the ties), a circle (ball) out of yellow felt, and so on.

Revolving Artwork Frames

A new baby in the house is very exciting. But older siblings need to feel special too. They'll want to make their presence known all over the house, including the nursery.

You can help him "share" that nursery in a peaceful and creative way. Put him in charge of some decorating details!

HERE'S WHAT YOU'LL NEED:

Art paper (8" x 10" or 9" x 12"), watercolors, pens, and pencils, and/or a collection of the older child's artwork

Colorful or plain white matting

Colored paper clips or wooden clothespins

Newspaper

Acrylic paints

Plate rack

Explain to your older child that rooms can look awfully bare without artwork and that you think his paintings would be great for the nursery. Add that it would be nice if the baby had something new to look at from time to time. He could do more as the baby grows!

Then watch him glow.

LET'S GET STARTED:

❧ Pull out the matting frame and select a painting from his ready-made collection, or he might like to paint something new.

❧ Slip the artwork between the front and back of the matting.

❧ Select colored clips to keep the matte "frame" snug around the artwork.

❧ If you want to paint the clothespins, spread them out on newspaper and paint away! Dots, stripes, squiggles! Anything goes. Allow the clips to dry fully before using.

❧ Accompany your child into the baby's room and help him decide where everything should go. Perhaps one on the dresser? Another on a shelf. Or display one on a plate rack.

Finally, encourage him to "show" the baby the fine art gallery now taking shape in the nursery! "Taylor," you might say as you hold baby Lily in your arms, "tell your sister about this one!"

"Baby and Me" Book

Everyone watches the baby for milestones. The first smile, the first giggle, the first time she sits up. But older kids are growing too. And often the new skills they develop are as exciting as those the baby displays. Why not write a book about it? What's the same? What's different? Your child will gain a better sense of his accomplishments and appreciate the baby steps we take as we grow.

HERE'S WHAT YOU'LL NEED:

Construction paper

Markers

Hole puncher

Ribbon or yarn

Photographs of each child

The first thing you'll want to do is "conduct an interview" with your preschooler about his skills and accomplishments. Can he count to 10? Does he sleep in a regular bed? Can he hop? Jot down what he has to say. Then put on your "publishing hat."

LET'S GET STARTED:

❧ On the top of a sheet of construction paper use markers to print, "My baby brother . . ." Finish the sentence with a fact noted earlier by your older child. For example, "My baby brother has one tooth." At the bottom of the page print a corresponding fact about the older sibling. "I have lots of teeth." Other examples might be, "My baby sister crawls. I can hop and skip." "My baby brother eats mashed bananas. I eat big hamburgers."

❧ Continue in this fashion for a number of pages and then end on a page where you note something the two children have in common. Examples might be: "My baby sister smiles. I smile too." Or, "My baby brother likes his blankie. I like my blankie too!"

❧ Illustrate the pages or cut out and glue pictures from a magazine together.

❧ Glue photographs of your children to the cover of the book and print the title: MY BABY SISTER AND ME.

❧ Punch holes along the left side of each sheet and weave the ribbon or yarn through, finishing it off with a bow. Now you've added a new book to your library! It makes for fine reading you can share time and again with your kids.

Secret Lunchbox Surprise

When my son was going off to kindergarten for the first time, I could tell he was awfully nervous about whether he'd make new friends. So to comfort him, I slipped into his lunchbox a photograph of us all on vacation in the Boundary Waters near Canada. The kids canoed and caught some fish. Well, one fish. Later the teacher told me that when he opened his lunchbox he broke into a huge smile and started telling everyone about his adventures. Presto! New friends!

Since then, I occasionally think up some surprise that can pick up their day.

HERE'S WHAT YOU'LL NEED:

Photographs of family members together during a fun time

Funny little notes

Fruit you can write on

Paper napkins

Markers

LET'S GET STARTED:

🖐 For younger kids, pop a photograph or loving little note on cards or napkins into their lunchbox.

🖐 For older kids, do it so no one will ever know but them! Write "Good Luck!" on a banana or orange, and once they get the message they can just peel it away. Quickly.

"G" Is for "Grandparents"

Family members sometimes live far away from each other. Or if they don't live that far apart, busy schedules keep them apart. Staying in touch can be tricky.

But it can also be fun. Especially if there's a game involved.

HERE'S WHAT YOU'LL NEED

Postcards

Pen/pencil

Stamps

Hole puncher

Large metal loop

Here's a new communication game. And it starts with a quest . . .

LET'S GET STARTED:

🖐 Explain to the kids and grandparents how you are going to be making a postcard alphabet book. (Actually you could explain the rules on the first postcard to Grandma and Grandpa.) Starting with your kids, find a postcard with a picture of something that begins with the letter "A."

🖐 Visit your local stationery or discount store and see what you can find. Or go to your post office and for the cost of a stamp buy a blank postcard on which your child can make a special drawing. Apple trees? Sure. Angels? Great! A lake? Well, save that for the "L" card. This is a great way for your young ones to learn the alphabet.

🖐 The kids can write or dictate a message.

🖐 Then the grandparents (or other recipient) of the "A" card should find a card with a picture of something that begins with the letter "B." Next, back to your kids. They've got to find "C": carrots, cars, chess.

🖐 Keep all the cards that are sent to your kids and have the grandparents keep all of theirs. At your next get-together, and after "Z" finally arrives, punch a hole in the corner of the cards and string them all on the loop in alphabetical order.

Then sit down together and enjoy it from "A" to "Z."

Grandparents adore getting these postcards. Being remembered and seeing a child's scrawl warms their hearts.

If Your Child Says, "I Don't Know What to Say!"

Suggest that one simple thought about the picture on the postcard will be nice. If she sent "C" for "cat," than maybe she'd like to write, "Grandma. I think this cat looks soft." If he sent "M" for "mountain," perhaps he can write, "Someday I want to climb this!"

Thank-You Postcards

Some grandparents have told me that there are times when they send a gift or write a note to a grandchild and it's as if it falls right into a black hole. Everyone's lives are so busy, and it seems that the simple acknowledgments that would mean so much may not happen.

It's not so easy to get kids to sit down to take the time to write a thoughtful note. There's always the baseball game going on outside, or a friend knocking on the door, or a basket full of action figures ready to distract. But not if you turn thank-you notes into an art project!

HERE'S WHAT YOU'LL NEED:

Blank cards or a drawing pad

Markers or crayons

Talk with your child about thanking Grandma and Grandpa for their present. A nice way is to draw them a picture of the gift. "That way," you might say, "they'll know for sure you got it and that you really like it."

LET'S GET STARTED:

🖐 You'll be amazed by how quickly your child sits down (she may run first for the gift to prop it up in front of her) to send proof of the present's arrival. Draw the gift with a marker, then color it.

🖐 When done, the simple words "Thank you for the baseball bat" scrawled on the other side will do nicely. If your child is young, let her dictate a message to you.

🖐 Then address, stamp, and mail the envelope.

Grandparents will be delighted by your child's effort and will end up with a terrific frameable piece of art to boot!

Audio Mail

There are certain voices in my life that I hear on the phone, or on my message machine that make me smile.

It hardly matters what is being said. The voices mean love.

A way to keep those voices in your ears is to send audiocassettes back and forth.

HERE'S WHAT YOU'LL NEED:

Blank audiocassettes

Tape player

LET'S GET STARTED:

❧ Pop a blank cassette into the tape player and let the spirit move you! Are you on a train with your kids? Have them describe to Grandma what they are seeing. "We're passing a farm! Look at that big black bull!" Are you tucking your little one into bed? Record the two of you reading a book together. Maybe your child would like to tell a few jokes.

❧ Then ask Grandma and Grandpa to do the same. Perhaps your children would like to send a tape asking questions about their grandparents' pasts. What was school like? Who were their best friends when they were in grade school?

This is a personal way to stay in touch, and best of all, these tapes can be saved. They can be listened to for years to come, keeping a part of ourselves always available to our loved ones.

Wearable Art

Here's an idea for including older siblings in the welcoming of a newborn. As the baby joins the family, the household may feel as if it's been turned upside down. But if you keep older children involved, they'll be part of the transition right along with you.

So sit down together and dress that baby with pizzazz!

HERE'S WHAT YOU'LL NEED:

Solid-colored or white 100 percent cotton baby outfit or T-shirts, freshly laundered to remove the sizing

Cardboard

Cookie cutters

Fabric paints in jars and squeeze bottles

Paper plate

Small foam paintbrushes or sponges clipped to clothespins

Pencil with eraser

You might say to the older sibling, "Let's design a special outfit for baby!"

LET'S GET STARTED:

❦ Slip a piece of cardboard in between the front and back of a prewashed cotton baby outfit. This will keep the paint from seeping through *and* help hold the painting surface flat.

❦ Choose a cookie cutter for a stencil. A star, moon, heart, duckling! Anything goes. Place it anywhere on the shirt.

❦ Pour a little permanent fabric paint onto a paper plate. Dip in the small foam paintbrush.

❦ Holding the cookie cutter firmly, start dab-dab-dabbing inside it, making sure to reach all the edges. You don't have to put equal density of paint all over the shape. A little variation actually adds interest.

❦ When you're through, lift the cookie cutter up to see the beautiful design. Now it's time for a few details.

❦ Dunk the eraser end of the pencil in a little paint. It can be the same color you used for the cookie-cutter shape or a completely different one. Then stamp it along the neck or sleeves for a fun, whimsical border.

❦ Add a few final details with the fabric squeeze bottles. You might want to write "Wee One" on the heart. Or maybe add a bow around the duck's neck!

❦ Let the outfit dry. Remove the cardboard, and if the paint bottles say to do so, now is the time to iron on the reverse side to set the color.

You're done. The baby is dressed, and his older sibling is feeling just grand!

QUICK TIP: Try a farm motif. Most particularly cow spots. Take an index card and draw cow spot shapes. Cut them out, and you have a simple stencil. Now lay it on the baby outfit, dip your brush in a little black or brown paint, and start dabbing. Then again, your kids might be more into dogs. Dalmatians, to be exact. So cut out smaller spot shapes, do the black paint routine, but add a little fire hydrant anywhere you'd like!

If Your Child Says, "Hmmm, This Is Nice—I Really Like Baby's Shirt"

Suggest that she make one for herself too. Pick up a plain white T-shirt at a discount or sporting goods shop. Then invite her to do a "grown-up" version of the baby's outfit. Hers could say, "Big One" or sport a beautiful swan. The same but different. Siblings, but each unique.

Family Picture Bio

Here's a way for your child to always have his family members at his fingertips. It's a chance to talk and think about them. Even the ones (and this I especially like) who live too far away for him to really "know."

"Is that Cousin Greg? He looks big! There's Grandpa in that favorite chair of his, and Uncle Bill with the baseball mitt forever stuck on his hand. Look at Grandma standing there in her light blue jogging suit."

Past and present pictures are fun too. "That's Great-grandma when she was little, skipping rope. Hmmm. There's Grandma hugging me now."

Your children will love having a fuller sense of the extended family—where they've come from and to whom they belong.

HERE'S WHAT YOU'LL NEED:

Photographs

Construction paper

Glue

Markers

Clear adhesive-backed paper

Hole puncher

Ribbon

LET'S GET STARTED:

❧ Select photos of family members. Color photocopy them if you don't wish to use the originals for this project.

❧ Paste each photo center stage on the page and label it. Include a caption if you'd like. "Uncle John when he had a beard."

❧ If you have past and present photos, you

might want to put them both on the same page and say, "Grandpa when he climbed his first tree!" and then, "Grandpa with me on his lap."

❦ Cover each page (both sides) with clear adhesive-backed paper. That way if sticky fingers smudge a page it can be wiped clean.

❦ Punch holes along the "spine" and weave in a ribbon. You can also opt to staple the pages together.

QUICK TIP: You might want to include a picture of your child, which can easily inspire delightful "family connection" conversation. "I think I look like Aunt Mary when her hair was long." "Gee, Uncle Bob loved baseball too!"

We share so much with our family members. And yet we're all so unique. We belong, but we each make our own way.

That's the wonderful message here.

Personal Photo Fest

Outtakes. Extras. Duplicates.
You know those "never did put them in an album" photos? The ones where kids are making faces? Or the ones that are almost exactly like the other, but not quite there? Or even good ones you just never framed?

Mine are in a big box. Or is it boxes?

Staring at the endless piles over the years, I've come up with all sorts of festive uses for them.

HERE'S WHAT YOU'LL NEED:

Old photos

Use of a photocopying machine

Glue

Big sheets of paper

Markers, glitter, feathers, rhinestones, etc.

LET'S GET STARTED:

This is an opportunity to use all your favorite and stray photos. Even the bloopers!

Photo Gift Wrap

🖐 Pick out a fun photo, go to the photocopy place, and make lots of copies. Then cut them out (or trim off any excess white paper) and glue them together in rows on a big sheet. Copy that.

🖐 With the markers, fill in some of the light spaces with bright colors to enhance the black and white. A little blue in the background. A green face or two! Maybe even a pink lake.

🖐 Gift-wrap a package and then cut this sheet to size and glue it on the front.

It's an Andy Warhol–like eye catcher!

Best Old Photo Invite

Is there an anniversary party coming up? Maybe it's Grandpa's seventieth?

🖐 If it's party time, pull out some old photos and pick a favorite appropriate to the event.

🖐 Copy the photo in black and

white and doodle it and color it and glitter it. Then glue it on blank note cards for invitations.

❧ Or enlarge the photo and glitz it up and use it as a poster at the party itself. Put it on a very large piece of tagboard and guests can pen in their messages below!

Surprise Birthday Portrait

❧ Enlarge one of your child's favorite pictures of himself to about 11″ X 17″ on a photocopying machine.

❧ Send it (in a tube) to each of the kids who are coming to the party and tell them in a brief note to "dress it up" any way they'd like. Paint it, add glitter and even pasta shapes, fasten ribbons, string rhinestones, fashion a headband . . . anything goes.

❧ When the guests arrive, have them secretly slip their "artistic interpretation" to you and then hang all of them up in a row on a wall.

❧ Finally, lead the birthday girl in to view her very personalized gallery! Pick a favorite "rendition" and frame it for her bedroom. (Check out the REVOLVING ARTWORK FRAMES activity so that she can rotate when she feels like it!)

QUICK TIP: *Use those bloopers!* Don't toss out the ones where the kids' eyes are closed but the dog looks cute . . . or you look great but the background is blurry. Cut out the parts you like. Create a collage on a piece of paper of the "saved" portions. Then photocopy and use for any of the suggestions above.

Note: Do not duplicate copyrighted photos from a professional photographer.

Video Reporter

Photographs are wonderful. But videotaping a person or family reunion adds an entirely new dimension to the ways in which we can replay a moment. It brings us closer. It allows us to see things we might have missed during the actual event.

A video camera can capture a gesture or laugh or familiar expression that speaks volumes about a person. And it gives kids a chance to feel closer to those people who live far away or who may not always be with us.

HERE'S WHAT YOU'LL NEED:

Video camera and blank tape

Script (optional)

Any time, any place

Clearly you can simply pick up a video camera and begin. However, I do think it's fun to encourage "the reporter" in every child.

LET'S GET STARTED:

🖐 Suggest that your child plan a script. What would he like to know about Grandma? What were her chores when she was young? Did she watch television? What was her mom like? Help him write out his questions and encourage younger ones to put in a few suggestions of their own.

🖐 If you're at a family reunion, discuss with your child how great it would be to make sure he captures *everyone* on tape . . . not just his favorite cousins! Call him a "roving reporter"!

🖐 Do be sure before the day is up to get the "reporter" on tape too. And ask him a few questions! "What was the most interesting part of the day?" "So, do you think television is in your future?" you might ask.

Finally, when all is quiet around the house, sit down with your family and watch the goings-on. You won't believe what you'll find out. "Hey, I didn't know Uncle John could throw a ball like that!" you might say. "Wow, Mom, what kind of dance was that you were doing with Aunt Judy?" your son might ask. Adding, with a big smile, "You know how to do that!?"

Videos are great for those moments you don't always see, as well as those you'd like to replay forever.

QUICK TIP: A tape recorder is another way to go. With script in hand, you can find out a lot. But spontaneous conversation is fun too. In fact, without a camera focused on their faces, sometimes people talk even more freely. "So, Grandma. What was Mom like when she was my age?"

GRAMPA'S 75TH BIRTHDAY

Table Talk

I t's always fun to distribute a little personalized surprise at mealtime. Individualized reading matter, to be exact. A well-timed comic strip on my husband's plate, an article on my daughter's favorite basketball player, or a movie review at anyone's place inspires wonderful mealtime conversation. It also keeps all of us aware of our many different interests and how much we can learn from each other!

HERE'S WHAT YOU'LL NEED:

Newspapers

Magazines

Postcards or letters from relatives and friends

Brochures or ads about places or things

Scissors

LET'S GET STARTED:

I enjoy this activity so much because it brings the family together as we share a piece of news or a funny cartoon, discuss a major sports event, or plan a dream vacation.

The truth is, however, I don't "get started." I get *inspired!*

I see something as I'm flipping through the paper or mail or a magazine and pull out the scissors. This will really give my son a kick, I think with a smile, as I snip out an article. Boy, will everyone enjoy this one, as I cut out a cartoon. Fun postcards or touching notes also get shared at dinner.

At my house the question "What's for dinner?" has come to mean a lot more than just food!

All it takes is, well, habit. It's one I hope I never shake.

A Mess a Minute

Kids love a good mess. And the "best of messes" often occur at inopportune times. Right before parties, directly after a bath, or on the way to school, church, or temple.

Well, I hit on an idea. One approach to messes is to give kids special *designated* times to really "mess it up." Maybe they need to not only be a mess but make the mess. After all, splashing in puddles or deciding to tackle each other in a pile of leaves is nature's ready-made mess waiting to happen.

GOOEY GOOP is good and messy and satisfying. It's usually accompanied by screams and squeals and a general atmosphere of mayhem. Then there are those activities that stir up a "natural mess." EDIBLE GARDENS are useful, artistic, and so wonderfully messy to finesse. It's a bit of "ick" with a delicious, earthy purpose. Perfect for both kids who don't mind getting some dirt under their fingernails and those who enjoy handling aromatic plants. And there's always the pleasure of homemade bubbles and, believe it or not, a unique way to make fun T-shirts with fish!

Let's face it. A mess is most often the sign of a good time.

So as parents, let's give ourselves a Medal of Honor for embracing a good grimy, gooey, gunky mess . . . and let the kids take it away!

In return, they might just make it to the party with clean shoes. Well, maybe.

Very Fishy Prints

Fish printing is a beautiful ancient art form using black ink and rice paper. If your kids love to fish, they too can make terrific prints with the day's catch, but if they are "hook and release" anglers, there's always the supermarket. You'll find the fish prints are not only lovely to look at but fascinating too. There's such exquisite and delicate detail in the scales along the body and on the fins. Suddenly what might have seemed like an ordinary fish will come colorfully alive in the most fascinating way.

HERE'S WHAT YOU'LL NEED:

Fish

Paper towels, cotton balls

Newspapers

Push pins

Several colors of acrylic or fabric paint

Paintbrushes (1"- to 1-½"-wide)

Clean cotton prewashed T-shirts, pot holders, pillow cases, aprons

LET'S GET STARTED

✸ Gently wash your fish and pat it dry with a paper towel. Stuff cotton balls or paper under the gills and lateral fins to absorb any excess moisture.

✸ Place the fish on a clean newspaper, an entire section folded in half. It should be able to hold the pins that keep the fish in place while there is a little give when you press down on the fish later.

✸ Using push pins to extend the fins will both secure the fish and create a more detailed print.

✸ Brush the fabric paint on the fish in one direction. (I tend to go sideways.) Be sure to paint the fins and tail. And feel free to use more than one color. There are rainbow fish, you know! One thing. Don't go too heavy on the paint because it may cloud the delicate detail of the fish and thus the print.

❤ Center the T-shirt (or apron or whatever) over the fish, then lay it down. Starting at the center of the fish, press the cloth on the fish and methodically move your hands from the center down, pressing, working toward the edges.

❤ Once you are finished pressing, gently peel the T-shirt or cloth from the fish and lay it out to dry. After the paint has dried, you might want to iron the shirt on the reverse side of the print to set the design.

QUICK TIPS: If paint gets on the newspaper as you are painting, quickly wipe it off to avoid unwanted stray markings on your T-shirt.

Also, glue or sew on a bead for the eye or rhinestones along the fins for a very glamour-fish look.

If your child's real fish print is a little undefined, use the squeeze and paint bottles to bring out the outline of the fish. Then have her add a few detailed scales for interest and color.

If you don't have a real fish, use a picture instead, then paint one on a T-shirt using squeeze and paint bottles. Prop up a picture of a fish in front of him so that he can use its basic shape as a guide. Then with regular acrylic paints, lightly fill in the center.

FOR EXTRA MEASURE:

Don't buy lots of fish for lots of tees! Your fish is reusable! Just paint over it again and again. I've used the same fish sixty times!

Gooey Goop

At one time or another I'm sure you've had some wild-colored gooey stuff take up residence in your home. It feels sticky, gets all over, and makes weird sounds. Qualities that kids enjoy most. Kids will rarely get tired of this activity. It's easy and quick. What could be better?

HERE'S WHAT YOU'LL NEED:

8-oz. bottle of household glue

Big bowl

8 oz. water

Poster paint or food coloring

Small bowl or measuring cup

1 c. warm water

1 ½ tsp. borax powder

Gather the family together and have fun as you proceed through this recipe for gooey goop. Once the stuff forms, you'll be amazed! Kids love it! Just keep it away from the carpets and upholstered furniture.

LET'S GET STARTED:

❧ Squeeze the entire bottle of glue into a big bowl. Then fill the empty glue bottle with water and add to the glue. Stir a lot.

❧ Add several drops of poster paint. You can mix colors or use just one. (I find that kids love the surprise of adding an extra color and seeing what emerges.)

❧ In the smaller bowl, stir together the cup of warm water and borax powder and stir until it's dissolved. Don't worry if you can't get all of the little clumps to disappear completely.

❧ Slowly, stirring constantly, pour the borax mixture into the glue mixture.

❧ Stir and swirl the results with your hands until the goop forms into gooey globs and starts slowly oozing from your slippery grasp. Kids will light up during this part.

Note: Right about now the dog will start chasing the cat and the mail carrier will arrive at the door asking for postage due. Never fails. It's the spirit of the gooey goop! *Chaos!*

QUICK TIP: If the gooey goop gets on your children's clothing, wash it out quickly with soap and water.

Sand Clay

Like most people, I enjoy taking long walks on the beach. I love the feel of sand under my feet and the way it stretches for miles before me. And then I suddenly feel inspired, thinking of the pounds and pounds of sand clay that could be made!

That's when I know it's time to go home and have some fun.

HERE'S WHAT YOU'LL NEED

1 c. clean sand

½ c. cornstarch

1 ½ tsp. powdered alum (available in the spice section of the grocery store)

½ c. water

Old cooking pot

Old wooden spoon

Sand Clay Plain and Simple

Get out those old kitchen utensils, and let's do some unusual cooking.

LET'S GET STARTED

🖐 Put all the ingredients into the pot and stir with your hands or a spoon.

🖐 An adult should place the pot on the stove, turn it to medium, and continue stirring.

🖐 As the mixture becomes warm, it will begin to liquefy. Continue to stir for two to three minutes more until the clay thickens.

🖐 Remove the pot from the heat and spoon the mixture out onto an old cutting board. Let cool.

🖐 Roll it into balls and make snow people, snakes, bowls, cars . . . anything! There are probably as many doable ideas as there are grains of sand between you and your kids' hands.

Sand Clay à La Decor

Dull frames? Lackluster mirrors?

Try a little sand clay, and you'll give has-been home accessories entirely new leases on life.

Creating with sand clay can be especially meaningful if you use old shells or pebbles gathered on family vacations. Suddenly something that was headed for the junk pile will become a treasured reminder of a wonderful family moment.

HERE'S WHAT YOU'LL NEED:

Picture frames or framed mirrors with wide edges

Damp sponge

Sandpaper

Paintbrush

Glue

Sand clay

Shells and pebbles

Clear acrylic spray (optional)

The next time you go to a garage sale, look for frames. A nickel here, a dime there, and you're all set!

LET'S GET STARTED:

🌑 Remove glass from any picture frames. You might have to leave the mirror the way it is, however. Then clean with a damp sponge and smooth over any rough spots in the wood with sandpaper.

🌑 Dip the paintbrush into *undiluted* household glue and spread it on the frame, one section at a time.

🌑 Stick a small clump of sand clay on the frame, pressing firmly.

🌑 If you have shells or pebbles, glue them directly on the frame and then, brushing more glue on the surrounding area, apply a little more sand clay.

🌑 Keep moving around the frame, pressing and molding.

🌑 Let the frame dry for a day or two.

🌑 If upon completion it occurs to you that a few more shells might be nice, just dunk them in the glue and press them right onto the sand clay frame.

🌑 If you wish, an adult can spray the frames (outside) with a light coat of clear acrylic paint.

🌑 Pick a favorite holiday snapshot, have it blown up if necessary, and pop it right in.

Just think. All this from something most people spend time sweeping *out* of their houses!

QUICK TIP: Here's an idea for **sandy triceratops party favors.** Mold the sand goop around plastic eggs containing little rubber dinosaurs. Let them dry a few days. At the end of the party pass one out to each child and invite them all to follow you to the sidewalk. Tell them to tap-tap-tap their eggs against the concrete. The eggs will break after a few tentative hits, and voilà! Your guests have just delivered a slew of baby dinos into the world! Perfect for a "birthday" favor.

Baking Soda Play Clay

This play clay is fun, clean, quick to make, easy to paint, and perfect for imaginative minds.

And of course, it's yet another chance to have a messy time!

HERE'S WHAT YOU'LL NEED:

Saucepan

2 c. baking soda

1 c. cornstarch

1-¼ c. water

Candy coloring (available at craft stores)

Acrylic paints and brushes

Grater

Garlic press

LET'S GET STARTED:

🐾 Place all the clay ingredients in a saucepan and stir it all up. An adult should cook the mixture on the stove over low heat for about 15 minutes, mixing all the while. Remove from the heat and continue stirring.

🐾 The mixture will take on a mashed potato consistency, and you'll soon have your play clay, soft and pliable and ready to use. At this point you can decide if you'd like to make a few colors by separating out the batches and adding a bit of candy coloring to each one.

🐾 Now it's time to sculpt. A basket of fruit is especially fun. Bananas with their long curvy shape are easy to mold. So are strawberries. Press your clay into a strawberry shape and then gently roll it up the side of a cheese grater to get that bumpy effect. For apple or pear stems, use a real stick or twig.

🐾 Maybe the kids are in a monster mode. So let them shape a face with eyes and mouth, then put a small lump of clay in the barrel of a garlic press and squeeze. Such long and lustrous hair! Just plop it on the monster head and press it gently down. Your child might prefer a serpent–frog–winged bat thing instead of a face. He'll enjoy creating whatever comes to mind!

🐾 Leave the creations out to air-dry. It should take about 12 hours.

🐾 Finally, if you haven't already colored your clay, paint the shapes with acrylic paints, adding details and designs.

If you make fruit, arrange your collection in a small wooden bowl for a mini-centerpiece. Display it at "teatime"!

QUICK TIP: Try a little bracelet of miniature "fruits." Mold some charm-size fruits, poke a hole in each one with a skewer, allow them to dry, and then paint on the details. String on a bit of elastic and enjoy a "fresh" accessory straight from the clay garden!

Edible Gardens

Beautiful things can emerge when you "dig right in!" A natural, glorious garden that just happens to be edible is a great place to start.

So scrunch that moss, let the soil run through your fingers, and press and pour and arrange until your basket runneth up and over.

HERE'S WHAT YOU'LL NEED:

Damp sphagnum moss from a garden store

Two big plastic containers

Small wire basket

Potting soil

Small potted herbs and edible flowers

Beautiful gardens aren't found only in backyards. They can be small (in pint-size milk cartons) and on wheels (in wagons) or carried in baskets. They can be interior decorations (in windows). And now you can plant your own!

LET'S GET STARTED:

✋ Place a good amount of moss in a big bucket or container. Everyone can gather around and, well, stick their hands right in. It's so nice and gushy handling the moss—kids will love it.

✋ Line a pretty metal wire basket with the moss, green side out. While you're working, place the basket in a large plastic container on the sink to catch dripping water. Press the moss up against the sides of the basket and all along the bottom. This will help the garden retain its moisture.

✋ Now scoop in the soil. I prefer the kind with a little vermiculite so that there's good drainage. Just fill the basket up with this soil to an inch or so below the top.

❧ Think about what you might like to plant. I love oregano, basil, and parsley. They are delicious on vegetables, salads, and pasta. Also choose an edible flower or two. Maybe colorful petunias and Johnny-jump-ups. The basket looks especially pretty when it has a bountiful look, so let the greenery just take over, spill out, and flourish everywhere.

❧ To help your garden along, water it and spritz it and soon you'll have the loveliest portable "plot" you could ever imagine. For presentation and watering purposes, place the basket in a large shallow clay pot.

QUICK TIP: As a trendy treat, not to mention a sophisticated surprise, serve up a long jelly roll or poundcake topped with a few dollops of whipped cream or a dusting of powdered sugar and a row of edible flowers resting along the length.

Then serve a flower with each slice.

A portable edible incredible garden. What fun!

Wacky Bubble Brew

Here you and the kids will be creating bubbles! You'll also be finding bubble makers, your own unique version of those simple little plastic ring sticks in a bottle. By the time you're done you'll be swimming in custom-made bubbles!

HERE'S WHAT YOU'LL NEED:

Large bowl

4 c. warm water

⅔ c. Joy liquid dishwashing detergent

1 Tbsp. glycerin

Long-handled spoon

Household items that have holes, won't get soggy, and don't have sharp edges—spatulas, plastic strawberry cartons, fly swatters, plastic six-pack holders, and anything else you can think of

You might want to surprise the kids with this, so don't let on exactly what this activity is.

LET'S GET STARTED:

🖐 Fill the big bowl with the water. Measure out the liquid detergent (please make sure it's not dish*washer* detergent) and add to the water.

🖐 Add the glycerin and stir a little more.

🖐 Pull out your junk box and the kitchen utensil drawer and say, "Everyone find a thing or two that won't get soggy in water and that has lots of holes in it!"

🖐 Go outside and give the kids a chance to guess what's going to happen. Maybe one will guess, maybe not. Then the moment of truth. . . .

🖐 Choose a bubble maker, dip it in the soapy liquid, and grandly wave it back and forth above your head while the bubbles fly!

QUICK TIP: Another kind of bubble maker, even quicker to make, is guaranteed to make everyone laugh. Pull out a washcloth. Get it nice and wet and then rub a bar of soap on one side. Then take the cloth, soapy side out, holding it kind of straight from two sides and place it over your mouth. Then blow. *Hard!* A cascade of little bubbles will form on the soapy side, spilling down, and cracking everyone up!

Pasta Pickup Sticks

Everyone's in the kitchen. Kids are hungry. But dinner isn't ready yet. They're starting to get very antsy. Surprise them by announcing, "Game time!"

HERE'S WHAT YOU'LL NEED:

Small fistful of uncooked regular-width spaghetti

Nice flat clean surface

Steady hands

You may recognize this game. It's just pickup sticks—with a pasta twist!

LET'S GET STARTED:

❧ Grasping the spaghetti in your fist, even it out by plunking the ends on the countertop.

❧ Holding it an inch or so above the counter, release your grasp and let the spaghetti fall where it may.

❧ Each child takes a turn trying to pick up a stick without moving the others. If they do disturb a stick other than the one they reach for, it's the next player's turn.

❧ Keep going until all the sticks have been picked up. The winner is the player with the most sticks.

QUICK TIP: Flat pasta like linguine limits the action!

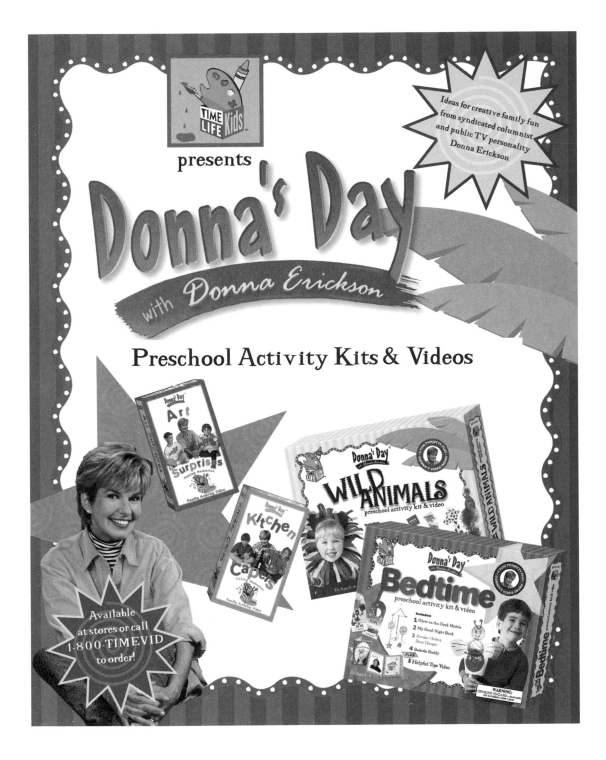